# STANLEY® COMPLETE
# DRYWALL

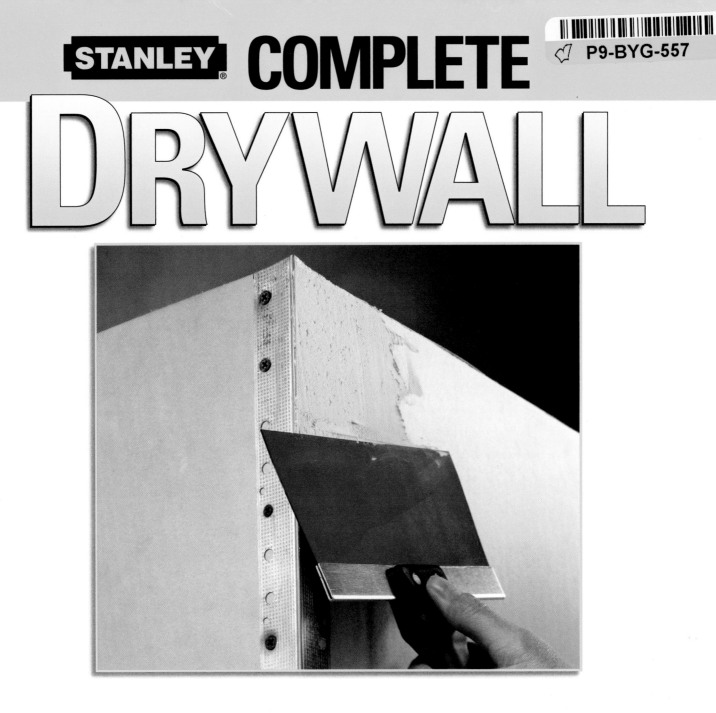

## WILEY

John Wiley & Sons, Inc.

**Note to the Readers:** Due to differing conditions, tools, and individual skills, the publisher assumes no responsibility for any damages, injuries suffered, or losses incurred as a result of following the information published in this book. Before beginning any project, review the instructions carefully, and if any doubts or questions remain, consult local experts or authorities. Because codes and regulations vary greatly, you always should check with authorities to ensure that your project complies with all applicable local codes and regulations. Always read and observe all of the safety precautions provided by manufacturers of any tools, equipment, or supplies, and follow all accepted safety procedures.

# CONTENTS

# A GUIDE FOR HOMEOWNERS AND REMODELERS

**W**hether you're a do-it-yourself novice or you're already the veteran of several remodeling projects, you'll discover information in this book that can preserve and even boost the value of your home.

Maybe you need to know how to fix gouged walls and a doorknob-sized hole before you paint. Perhaps you've wondered how to repair a sagging ceiling. Or, you've dreamed of making your house live larger by converting a wasted attic, garage, or basement into enjoyable living space. Whether your goals are modest or ambitious, you've selected the right guide for your project.

### How the book is organized
The book opens with a gallery of great-looking rooms to serve as a springboard for your imagination. You'll see how you can utilize drywall to create inviting interior spaces that range from purely functional to highly decorative.

Next, you'll get solid advice on choosing exactly the right materials and selecting the correct tools to bring your project to life.

The chapter on framing gets your project off on the right foot. It includes the basics of wall construction and incorporates helpful special topics such as building soffits and how to craft a curved wall. You'll learn traditional wood carpentry as well as the advantages steel studs offer.

You'll see how to plan your drywall job, and you'll also begin to master the material, making simple straight cuts as well as cutouts for electrical boxes and ceiling fixtures. You'll learn all the processes in a drywall project: hanging, taping, mudding, and sanding. And if you want to try your hand at advanced techniques, you'll find solid advice and helpful hints.

### The book's format
This book packs dozens of how-to photo sequences across the top of the pages. This format reduces even complicated topics into small steps that you'll quickly understand and put to work.

In addition to the how-to advice, the book also covers the whys behind each process. The bottom half of each spread packs valuable advice on the reasons behind each technique. You'll discover helpful advice on special techniques and Pro Tips to make your job go faster and give you better results.

### You can do it
Even if you're an absolute novice at drywall, you can enjoy good results right from the start when you have the knowledge at your fingertips to guide you confidently step by easy step to completion.

Exercise some patience, and you can achieve great results. Sometimes, the only thing that separates acceptable workmanship from the truly superior is the willingness to inspect more carefully and invest the time for one more application of compound and one more thorough sanding.

# ELEMENTS OF STYLE

If your walls and ceilings could talk, you might hear a cry for help. They would probably begin with a heart-to-heart conversation about the bumps, dings, and scrapes they've suffered at the hands of an active family. But then the discussion would probably turn to the fact that they long to be treated as more than merely utilitarian surfaces, that they can be decorative and expressive.

Consider an average room as a six-sided geometrical figure and then count the number of surfaces covered by drywall: four walls and the ceiling. In fact, if your home is like most built during the past 40 years, drywall is the predominant visible interior surface.

An artist or sculptor would consider these extensive surfaces of your home as opportunities for creative expression and decorative treatment.

But economic realities dictate that contractors produce affordable housing, not works of art. That usually means choosing construction methods that promote speed at the expense of style.

As a homeowner with a do-it-yourself inclination, you can invest the extra time and effort that makes drywall a medium of self-expression—not merely a surface that covers the framing. So instead of hanging pictures to convey personality, use the walls and ceilings themselves to express your style.

When you consider drywall this way, you'll see that raised panels can be part of a real character-building program for your home. A generic wall can become a decorative wainscot, or a popcorn ceiling will give way to a raised-panel treatment or even undergo a sculptural makeover.

Curved walls can give old rooms a new vitality. And a curved soffit can define functional areas within an open floor plan, eliminating the need to chop up the space by constricting walls.

You can continue the curves with drywall arches. Though they require more initial effort than a ho-hum rectangular doorway, arches eliminate the need for expensive trimwork, not to mention the miter-cutting hassles, messy staining, and tedious finishing required for moldings.

Listen to your walls and ceilings, and answer their call for help. When you're finished, they will speak eloquently of your good taste.

**You can transform drywall into a medium of expression—not merely a surface that covers the framing.**

## CHAPTER PREVIEW

**Decorative drywall**
*page 8*

**Curved drywall**
*page 10*

**Arched drywall**
*page 11*

**Imaginative ceilings**
*page 12*

*From ceiling to floor, this room is transformed by the creative use of drywall. The paneled ceiling elevates the level of sophistication; the graceful curved arches define the space and showcase the fireplace and windows.*

**Medallions**
*page 14*

# DRYWALL GOES DECORATIVE AND DRAMATIC

Think outside of plain boxy shapes and you'll energize your rooms with interesting angles or the classic great looks of raised-panel construction. Drywall construction techniques put these great effects and many other imaginative solutions well within your reach.

A fireplace makes an interesting case study because the usual impulse is to center it along a wall. Although it's sometimes an acceptable solution, that thinking is a holdover from the days when the hearth was the primary source of heat as well as the cook's headquarters.

**Getting a new angle on the solution**

Relocating the hearth to the corner of the room is an imaginative solution that definitely puts a fireplace in its place. It remains architecturally important in the room without completely overwhelming your decorating options. Lighting built in above the artwork casts a soft glow without drawing attention to its source.

Drywall and its framing weigh a fraction of a brick and mortar fireplace, so that eliminates the need for expensive structural supports. And if you tackle the project yourself, you can also save a ton of money.

**Panels raise your interest level**

Because of the high cost of materials and especially the highly skilled labor required, raised-panel walls have always been limited to upscale homes. Until now.

An innovative drywall product with a molded pattern eliminates the need for fancy carpentry work. Instead, you provide basic drywall installation and finishing techniques.

You'll find raised-panel drywall that's scaled for installation on upper walls, wainscots, stairways, and even ceilings. Although you'll be tempted to fill every square foot of your room with these great-looking panels, it's a good idea to control your enthusiasm. Too much of a good thing can simply be too much.

*Angle a fireplace into a corner, and you'll open up options for decorating and furniture arrangement. Fire-resistant drywall and steel studs are a natural combination for this project, but always check local building codes to ensure safe construction.*

*Raised-panel drywall transforms a wainscot from ordinary to extraordinary without breaking your budget. You'll also be pleased that a do-it-yourselfer can manage the installation.*

*Take the raised-panel treatment to new heights by installing an upper wall treatment as well as a wainscot. The panels have an identical width, but those on the upper wall are taller.*

*Compare the two photos at the bottom of this page, and you'll discover that a raised-panel wainscot can be right at home with a variety of decorating styles. Above, muted colors convey understated elegance.*

*Shift your paint palette, and your wainscot takes on an entirely new flavor. The decorating possibilities are endless—especially if you enjoy experimenting with faux painting techniques.*

# CURVED WALLS ARE EASIER THAN EVER TO BUILD

You may well wonder how you can start with straight studs and flat sheets of drywall and end up with smoothly sweeping curves. But even though the results may seem magical, creating curves is a straightforward process. In fact, with the introduction of an innovative segmented track, building a curved wall has never been easier or more certain.

Curves have an undeniable universal appeal because they mimic the flows and rhythms of nature far more gracefully than straight lines and stark angles ever can.

### Curves demand careful planning

As you might suspect, a curved wall is a bit more difficult to construct than a flat wall, but you'll discover that the process is more a matter of careful planning than mysterious or difficult techniques. In fact, the chapter "Framing for Drywall" contains an easy stud-spacing chart that will help ensure your curved wall is both smooth and sturdy. The accompanying photo sequence shows you every step in building a wall. The other key piece of information you'll need is the chart of minimum bending radii for various thicknesses of drywall. You'll find that handy table on *page 110*. It's exhaustively complete, giving you the minimum curve achievable for all standard thicknesses applied both wet and dry, bent across both length and width.

Again, you'll see a step-by-step demonstration that removes every bit of uncertainty from the techniques that you'll use. The scale of the project doesn't change your method of work—only the scale of the pieces. So you'll utilize a similar approach to craft a curved soffit, a half-wall, a full-height wall, or even a curved staircase.

With all of the data charts and technique reference material at your fingertips, you'll find that it's not a difficult learning curve.

### Tear down this wall

After you've satisfied yourself about the "how" of curved walls, you'll begin looking around your house to see exactly where you can build one.

If your home has a choppy floor plan that you'd like to open, consider tearing down some full-height walls and marking the boundaries of activity areas with a curved half-wall. Take the concept one step further and eliminate the walls, utilizing a curved soffit as a visual cue to define areas without enclosing them. This soffit suggestion is particularly apt for a basement remodel. You'll probably need to build a soffit anyway to conceal utility runs, so make the architectural feature also serve decorative and boundary roles.

### Pitching even more curves

As you start thinking more about curves, you'll discover new possibilities around every corner.

Between your kitchen and family room, for example, consider a new counter with undulating edges atop a wavy half-wall. Or transform a homely kitchen soffit into a curvaceous beauty.

But don't limit your imagination to only curves along vertical planes. After all, a barrel-vaulted ceiling is simply a curved wall that's been relocated. So as you're looking around for creative opportunities, don't forget to also look up.

*Although you probably couldn't duplicate this idea at full scale in your home, this photo illustrates how a curved ceiling structure defines functional areas while eliminating walls. It's a great idea for opening up your floor plan in both living and recreational areas of your home.*

*The drywall-clad sides of this staircase give it a sculptural presence. For a project as ambitious as this, you may want to consider contracting the framing and then handling the drywall phase yourself.*

# ARCHED DRYWALL OPENS NEW DESIGN VISTAS

If you're ready to give your home a design element with enduring good looks, consider the classic arch. Examples built during the Roman Empire survive to this day, and they still never fail to delight the eyes of tourists.

Although the Roman engineers often chose the arch for structural reasons, your arch will probably skip the heavy lifting and concentrate on style.

### Make a bold opening statement

Framing an arched opening is a job that's well within the range of the do-it-yourself enthusiast. And doing your own construction is more than a money-saving strategy. It also allows you to customize the opening exactly the way you want it.

For example, you can design an arch that echoes the sweep of a favorite cabinet or piece of furniture. See the photo at right to see how the curves in wood and drywall reinforce each other. You'll also see repeating architectural curves in the photo below. Notice how the arched opening in the foreground mirrors the shape of the bow-top window in the distance.

### Explore even more possibilities

Modern drywall tapes and beads offer several design choices. The familiar square-edge bead produces crisp corners that have a contemporary look. But you can also choose bullnose beads in several radii for a softer, more flowing appearance.

Many arches represent true circular segments, but there's no law that prohibits you from exploring parabolic shapes, catenary curves, elliptical segments, multi-axis arches, and even asymmetrical openings. Go for it.

*The arched opening in the foreground wall echoes and reinforces the graceful shape of the bow-top window in the background.*

*Here is another example of theme and variation. The arched opening repeats the shape of the arbor-like top. Even though the materials and treatments are different, your eye immediately recognizes the similarities of shape and rhythm.*

# IMAGINATIVE CEILINGS

**C**eilings are far too often like Midwestern farm country—a monotonous expanse that serves a useful function but accomplishes it with little, if any, variation or creativity. Whether it's popcorn texture or cornfields, once you've seen a little, you've seen enough.

Drywall makes it easy to banish boring ceilings by incorporating raised-panel designs or creating sculptural elements.

**Designs can be structure or sculpture**

The design of a ceiling can reflect a home's structural framing or be purely decorative.

The soaring "tepee" ceiling shown below right is an example of functionally based design, while the fanciful shape at right is more sculpture than structure. Both require careful workmanship—certainly not beyond homeowner skills—to maintain smooth runs of crisp angles.

Raised-panel ceilings also require careful planning to ensure that the overall design is centered in the room. You'll find comfort in mapping out the grind in advance, which will ensure that the edges of the design line up in both directions. You can fill in the edges of the ceiling with ordinary drywall to eliminate partial panels at the perimeter.

*Precise workmanship paid huge dividends in the creation of angles that are simultaneously free-flowing and crisp. Careful construction of the underlying framing was another crucial component.*

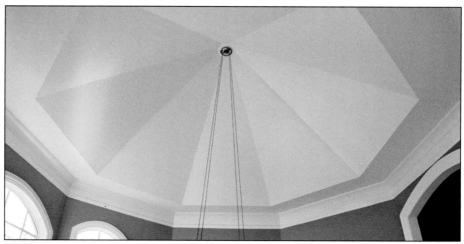

*A successful "tepee" ceiling requires attention to symmetry.*

*Linear regularity—from wainscot to windows—is this room's dominant theme, making a raised-panel ceiling the perfect crowning touch. If your ceiling paint has even a hint of gloss, you'll need to exercise special care in sanding every seam to a flawless finish.*

# MEDALLIONS ARE THE FAST TRACK TO AN UPSCALE IMAGE

Ceiling medallions were once found only in extremely upscale environments like the old motion picture palaces and in the private residences of the socially elite. There was a simple reason for that: You had to be wealthy to afford the time and talents of a master plaster craftsman.

But modern plastics technology excels at reproducing rich detail, slashing weight, and making an extremely expensive item very affordable. And perhaps best of all, the skill component has virtually disappeared.

### Choices, choices, and more choices

No matter the architecture and decorating style of your room, you'll find a medallion that's just your style. The spectrum ranges from the fantastically floral designs typical of Victorian taste to simple lines that complement modern decor.

Selecting the right size of medallion is another important step. As a general guideline, choose a medallion with a diameter that equals or slightly exceeds the greatest diameter of the lighting fixture that will be beneath it. If the medallion is too small, it will make the fixture appear incongruously large. And a jumbo medallion will dwarf your light fixture. The Goldilocks

principle applies here: not too big and not too small but just right.

Ceiling fans and large chandeliers are two examples when the guideline doesn't apply. In those instances, simply select a large medallion—in the 24- to 36-inch range.

### Installation is fast and easy

Many medallions have a 4-inch central hole to match the typical ceiling electrical box. If you're not using the medallion where you need the hole, filling it is literally a snap. Simply pop in a rosette (usually sold separately) in a matching style.

The chapter "Decorative Finishes" includes a photo essay that details the easy steps involved in a medallion's installation. In fact, you'll spend most of your time removing and reinstalling the light fixture. If electrical work isn't one of your strengths, you have several choices: hire an electrician, select a split-ring design, or choose a centerless ring that you can maneuver around the fixture without removing it.

Ceiling medallions and other polyurethane products accept paint well. If you're applying a faux finish, you'll find it easier to complete those steps prior to installation.

### Complementary products

Manufacturers also utilize polyurethane for a wide range of other decorative products, including fireplace mantels, door surround kits, precast wall niches, molding strips, and even crown moldings.

To make the crown molding even easier to install, you'll also find inside and outside corner blocks that eliminate the need for tedious coping and mitering.

*The medallion's diameter should equal or be slightly larger than the light fixture.*

*For a regal look, customize medallions and moldings with ordinary paint or a faux finish.*

*This room is a polyurethane tour de force, featuring a medallion, niche, crown molding, field molding, door surround, and chair rail.*

*Unless you tap the moldings with your fingernail, you'd never know that they are plastic instead of plaster. The medallion, niche, fireplace, and doorway surrounds all demonstrate the material's ability to reproduce rich detail.*

*Snap in a coordinating rosette to close up the standard 4-inch central hole in a medallion.*

*Medallions for ceiling fans abandon the guideline for equal size for both fixture and the ceiling decoration.*

# MATERIALS & SUPPLIES

**M**ost people think drywall is a generic product that offers a limited number of choices: a couple of thicknesses and a few different lengths. But even if you've already heard about fire-rated and moisture-resistant panels, you may not know about sag-resistant ceiling panels, abuse-resistant sheets, and foil-backed panels. You'll also discover special bending drywall as well as sound-control panels, backerboard, and even dimensional products that mimic the raised-panel look.

### Fasteners, tapes, and beads

Selecting the drywall itself is only part of the process. For a sturdy and long-lasting installation, you'll also need to choose fasteners that are compatible with the panel's thickness and the type of framing, either wood or steel studs. You'll even discover the correct screw-thread pattern for a variety of applications. Having the right tapes and beads for your project can make it relatively easy to get smooth seams and crisp corners—even if you're a beginner. And while you're buying your supplies, pick up a few patch kits. They transform mistakes, such as a miscut electrical box, from a catastrophe into a minor inconvenience.

## Spending extra time to select top-quality materials prevents frustration in the long run.

### CHAPTER PREVIEW

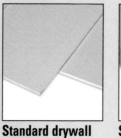
**Standard drywall panels**
*page 18*

**Specialty panels**
*page 20*

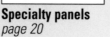
**Fasteners**
*page 22*

**Drywall tapes**
*page 24*

A successful drywalling project requires some up-front planning, including estimates of the amount of materials needed. This chapter will help you choose the right materials, so a shopping trip to the lumber yard or home center will assemble all you need to start and finish your work.

**Drywall
compounds**
*page 26*

# STANDARD DRYWALL PANELS

**S**tandard drywall panels have tapered edges and are manufactured in 8-, 9-, 10-, 12-, and 14-foot lengths. The exception is ¼ drywall, available only in 8- and 10-foot lengths.

The **½-inch panel** is the most common thickness of drywall and is generally utilized in single-layer applications on residential walls and ceilings. It can also be used in multilayer applications for improved sound control *(page 21)*.

In **⅜-inch thickness,** the panel has reduced weight and is usually applied in double layers in new construction. In remodeling, you can utilize the thinner panel over existing surfaces to create a fresh and flat surface.

The **¼-inch panel** is also useful as an overlay for walls and ceilings in remodeling projects. It bends easily to create archways and curved walls, although its bending radius is not as small as ¼-inch flexible drywall. Refer to the chart on *page 120* for minimum bending radii for a variety of panels.

**¼-inch flexible drywall**
This specialty product is very useful for creating tight-radius archways and curves in walls and ceilings. The tapered-edge panel is 48 inches wide, and you can buy it in 8- and 10-foot lengths.

**54-inch-wide panels**
By utilizing panels that are 54 inches wide, you can apply drywall horizontally to walls that are up to 9 feet tall. Horizontal application produces a stronger wall. You'll

¼-inch drywall: Good for curved surfaces

⅜-inch drywall: Good for covering old walls and some curves

## Transporting drywall

Drywall is heavy and not very strong, particularly when it is unsupported. If you try to transport a stack propped up on a tailgate or otherwise wedged into a car or van, the bottom sheets may break. To avoid such trouble, place a couple of 2×4s underneath to add support. Another concern: The weight of a big stack may damage your vehicle. Make two or more trips if necessary, or have it delivered.

find these wide panels in ½- and ⅝-inch thickness and in lengths of 8, 9, 10, 12, and 14 feet. Vertical application helps minimize hard-to-conceal butt joints (the junction of two untapered edges).

**Fire-resistant drywall**
Building codes specify where you must use fire-resistant drywall—furnace rooms and attached garages are typical examples. The typical panel chosen for these applications is ⅝ **inch thick,** and carries an X fire-resistance designation. At least one manufacturer makes a ½-inch panel with special additives in the gypsum core (designated C core) that improves its fire resistance above that provided by the ⅝-inch panel. Carefully check with your local building inspection department to ensure that your materials and construction methods comply with regulations.

Even when you don't need fire-resistant properties, ⅝-inch drywall is a great choice. In fact, it's your best choice for the highest quality results in a single-layer application throughout your home. The slightly thicker panels produce significant improvements in several important areas at only a modest price increase over ½-inch drywall. The thicker panes produce walls and ceilings that are flatter, more sag resistant, don't dent as easily, control sound better, and span wider framing (chart on *page 45*).

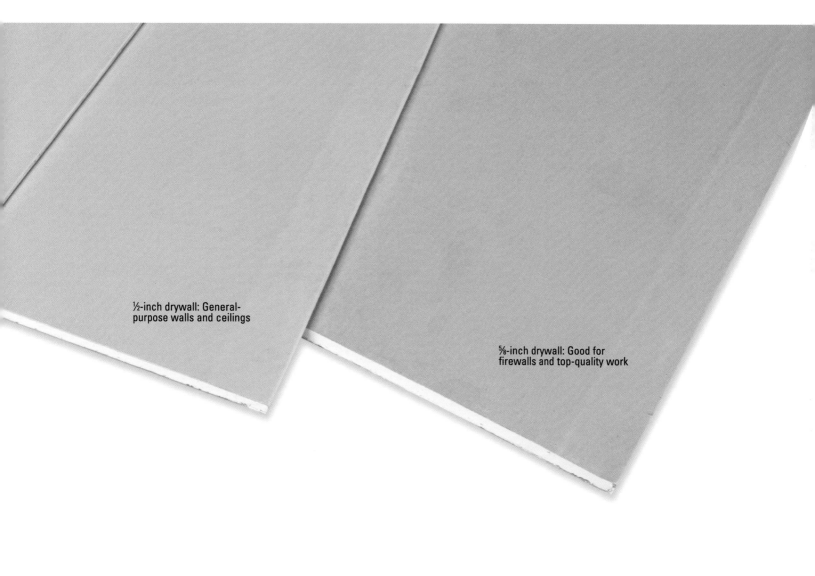

½-inch drywall: General-purpose walls and ceilings

⅝-inch drywall: Good for firewalls and top-quality work

# SPECIALTY PANELS

### Moisture-resistant drywall

You can easily identify moisture-resistant drywall by its distinctive green, blue, or blue-green color. Some typical application areas include bathrooms and kitchen backsplashes. It accepts paint and wallpaper and serves as an acceptable base for ceramic and plastic wall tiles in areas that will not be wet for a prolonged time (walls other than a tub surround, for example). However, if you utilize it as a tile substrate, you should omit the installation of a vapor barrier behind the panel. The material is not waterproof and will not tolerate constant moisture or humidity.

Moisture-resistant panels are available in $\frac{1}{2}$- and $\frac{5}{8}$-inch thicknesses and also in fire-resistant panels: a $\frac{1}{2}$-inch thickness with a C designation and $\frac{5}{8}$-inch thickness rated X. The 48-inch-wide panels have tapered edges and are available in 8-, 10-, and 12-foot lengths.

### Abuse-resistant drywall

For increased dent resistance, consider abuse-resistant panels. You can use them as an upgrade in virtually any room in the house. Likely locations include garages, recreation rooms, a child's room, high-traffic hallways, workshops, and hobby rooms.

The panels are available in $\frac{1}{2}$-inch or $\frac{5}{8}$-inch thickness with an X fire-resistance rating. The tapered-edge panels are 48 inches wide and available in 8-, 10-, and 12-foot lengths.

### Sag-resistant ceiling panels

Ordinary drywall panels can deform under the weight of insulation or sag when softened by the application of texturing or finishing materials. One way to overcome these problems is to upgrade to $\frac{5}{8}$-inch panels, but their weight can make installation difficult. Sag-resistant $\frac{1}{2}$-inch-thick panels offer a solution without creating a weight problem. The tapered-edge panels are 48 inches wide and come in 8- and 12-foot lengths.

### Foil-backed panels

These panels are essentially standard drywall with a kraft-backed aluminum foil laminated to the back face, useful in cold

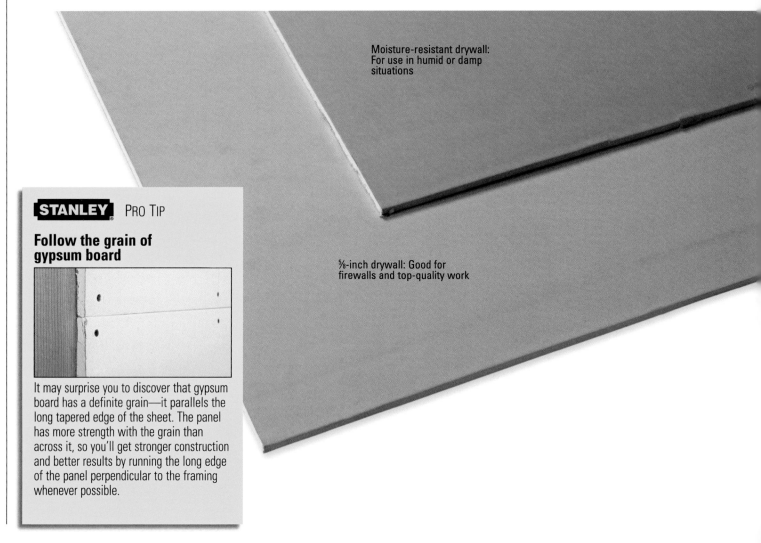

Moisture-resistant drywall: For use in humid or damp situations

$\frac{5}{8}$-inch drywall: Good for firewalls and top-quality work

---

**STANLEY** PRO TIP

### Follow the grain of gypsum board

It may surprise you to discover that gypsum board has a definite grain—it parallels the long tapered edge of the sheet. The panel has more strength with the grain than across it, so you'll get stronger construction and better results by running the long edge of the panel perpendicular to the framing whenever possible.

climates. By installing the metal face against the framing in a single- or multilayer application (foil-backed for the base layer only), you create a vapor barrier that prevents the migration of moisture into wall or ceiling spaces.

The panel is not recommended as the base for ceramic or other tiles. You should also not use these panels in air-conditioned houses when the area has sustained heat and humidity, such as in the Southern Atlantic or Gulf Coast regions of the United States. Check with a mechanical engineer (heating/cooling specialist) if you have doubt about the installation of these panels in your climate zone.

Spaces with extreme conditions—especially high moisture levels, such as an indoor hot tub or pool, sauna, or steam room—demand special solutions. Consult a drywall supplier or mechanical engineer for material recommendations.

You should also consult an expert for advice in achieving high levels of noise reduction or fire resistance.

A special gypsum panel called blueboard is used as the base under veneer plaster applications, and redecorated panels are often used in factory-built housing such as mobile and modular homes. However, these products are outside the scope of this book.

### Sound control and backerboards

**Sound control board** (Homasote 440 is one brand) is installed as the first course in a multilayer installation. The panel is manufactured from cellulose fiber and offers thermal insulation plus sound reduction when installed in floors and ceilings.

The product is manufactured in thicknesses of ½, ⅝, and ¾ inch.

**Gypsum backerboard** is available in several thicknesses, and is utilized as a substrate for installation of ceramic tile and stone on both walls and floors. You can score and snap gypsum backerboard just as you do with drywall panels.

As its name implies, **cementious backerboard** is a cement product that's reinforced with a fiberglass mesh. Cutting this product is more difficult than its gypsum cousin, but it can be more durable if subjected to water. You'll find this product in several thicknesses.

Both types of backerboard require special corrosion-resistant screws—ordinary drywall screws are NOT recommended. Also make certain that you purchase fiberglass mesh tape that's compatible. The drywall variety of tape is not suitable.

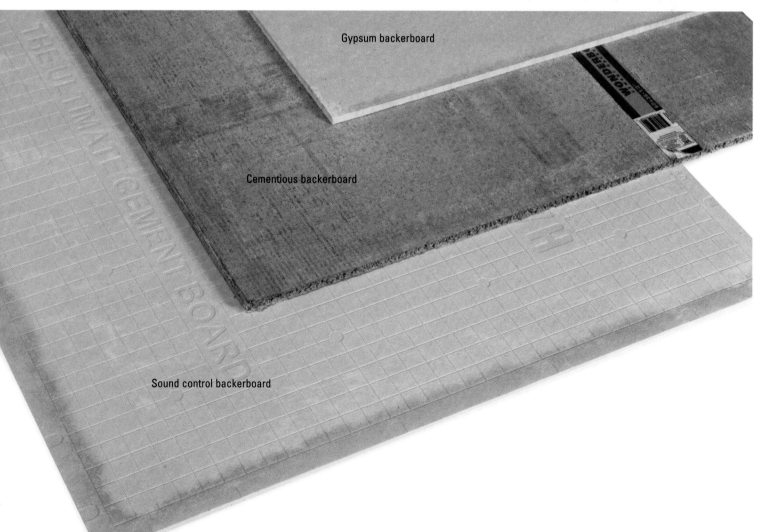

Gypsum backerboard

Cementious backerboard

Sound control backerboard

# FASTENERS

Nails driven into wood split apart wood fibers, and the friction between the nail's shank and the wood gives the fastener its holding power. Although you can purchase **smooth-shank drywall nails,** those with annular rings (commonly called **ringshank**) have up to 20 percent more holding power for virtually the same price. Although that may sound like a modest increase in strength, it can make the difference between a smooth wall and one that develops unsightly nail pops.

The vast majority of professional drywallers now choose screws because they have up to 3½ times the pullout resistance of nails. That translates into far fewer popped fasteners.

**Longer is not necessarily better**
The prime culprit causing nail pops is framing lumber that has too high a moisture content. As the lumber shrinks (principally in width) during drying, it pulls away from the drywall while the nails try to stay in the same position. When the lumber's movement is stronger than the nail's grip, the nail pops.

Somewhat surprisingly, attempting to prevent the problem by using longer nails for the installation simply makes the situation worse. The deeper you go into lumber, the higher its moisture content, and the more the nail moves when the wood dries. As a result, long nails pop more than short ones.

The best prevention is to use a fastener that produces adequate holding power with minimal lumber penetration. Refer to the chart (opposite right) to choose ringshank nails. Or even better: Select screws when driving into new lumber.

Nail pops are less of a problem in a remodeling project when you're hanging drywall on well-seasoned framing lumber. To cure nail pops, refer to *page 138*.

**Essential fasteners**
Annular ring drywall nails offer good pullout resistance in wood. Smooth-shank nails aren't recommended; they work out easily.

**Type W bugle head screws** have a coarse thread pattern that gives excellent holding power in wood framing.

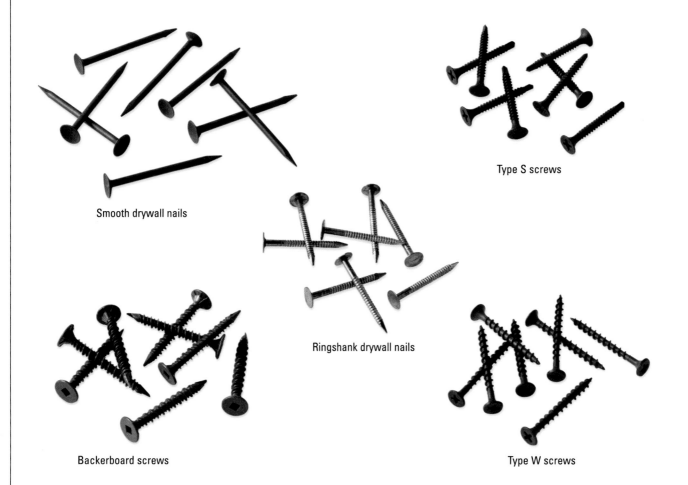

Smooth drywall nails

Type S screws

Ringshank drywall nails

Backerboard screws

Type W screws

**Type S bugle head screws** have a tip that drills its own hole in metal studs and other steel framing members. The fine thread pattern is designed for maximum gripping power in metal. Some type S screws have a high/low thread design like the trim head screw for slightly faster driving.

Type G laminating screws have a large diameter and coarse threads for holding power when driven into gypsum board. This allows you to build multilayer applications without driving fasteners into the framing. The base layer must be at least ½-inch thick when using these screws.

Trim head screws attach door jambs, baseboards, and other moldings to drywalled surfaces over metal studs.

The modified truss head screw is the special fastener for joining metal studs to tracks *(page 47)*.

**Backerboard screws** are made from stainless steel or from steel with a special corrosion-resistant coating. The stainless-steel screw shown here has nibs under the head that cut a countersink in cementious backerboard so that the head is flush.

**Drive systems**
The most-used drive system for drywall screws is the cruciform (cross-shaped) #2 phillips. It's an efficient and time-proven design, but it won't work properly if your drive bit is worn, rounded, or chipped. Replace the bit at the first sign of wear. The phillips ACR bit has ribs that resist the tendency of the bit to lift out of the slot (cam out) under driving stress. When you use an ACR bit, you reduce the need to supply as much downward pressure to keep the bit engaged.

Square drive (sometimes called Robertson) screws are even more resistant to camout. The drive and recess have such tight tolerances that you can achieve a "stick fit"—where the fastener won't fall off the bit regardless of position. However they are more difficult to load onto the bit than phillips heads. Trim head screws typically have a #1 square recess; #2 square is more common on construction screws.

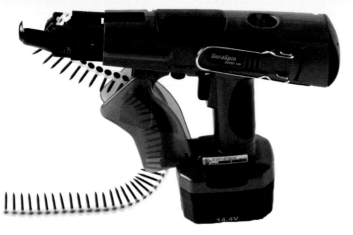

Self-feeding screwgun

## FASTENER SELECTION GUIDE

The following chart guides you in the selection of the right fastener for hanging drywall. For multilayer applications, choose a fastener that's appropriate for the layer you're installing. For example, if you're installing a double layer of ½-inch drywall onto wood studs, you'd use 6 × 1¼-inch screws to apply the first layer and 6×1⅝-inch screws for the second.

| Drywall thickness (1) (inches) | Nails into wood (length in inches) | Screws into wood (length in inches) | Screws into steel (2) (length in inches) |
|---|---|---|---|
| ¼, ⅜ | 1¼ | 6 x 1¼ | 6 x 1 |
| ½ | 1¼ | 6 x 1¼ | 6 x 1 |
| ⅝ | 1⅜ | 6 x 1¼ | 6 x 1 |
| ¾ | 1½ | 6 x 1⅜ | 6 x 1¼ |
| ⅞ | 1⅝ | 6 x 1½ | 6 x 1⅝ |
| 1 | 1¾ | 6 x 1⅝ | 6 x 1⅝ |
| 1¼ | 2 | 6 x 2 | 6 x 1⅝ |

*Notes: (1) This column refers to the total thickness of drywall and includes multilayer applications. (2) Steel includes metal studs, resilient channels, and similar residential-grade materials.*

# DRYWALL TAPES

There are two basic types of joint tape: paper and fiberglass mesh. The **flexible paper tape** usually has a seam running along its width to make it easy to crease for installation into an inside corner. Paper tape is more time consuming to install because it has to be embedded into a coat of compound. And if you embed it incorrectly, the paper can blister or wrinkle, forcing a repair.

**Fiberglass mesh tape** is usually self-adhesive, although you may encounter a nonadhesive variety that is far less convenient because it requires staples to hold it in position. Installing fiberglass tape along inside corners can be a challenge unless you have a special application dispenser *(page 37)*.

Backerboard requires a special type of fiberglass tape that resists deterioration from the chemicals in thinset mortar.

### Composite and metal tapes

Applying joint compound to inside corners can be a challenge because you need to create a straight line with joint compound. Composite and metal tapes help you get sharp corners, even if you're a drywall novice. The folded tape creates a crisp line, and you simply need to blend the thickness of the tape into the surrounding walls to make the product disappear.

There is also a special composite tape that helps you create smooth curves and arches (see *page 102* for installation details). These rolled tapes are ideal to create straight or curved outside corners.

### Beads and specialty items

You'll find a wide variety of materials for creating outside corners. You can hammer or clinch metal bead into place, nail vinyl beads, and embed composite and paper-covered metal beads.

If you get involved in a big job, you'll really speed the work by buying or renting a hopper. You simply load the hopper with all-purpose nonsetting compound and push in a length of bead. Adjustable rubber gates control the amount of compound that's applied as you pull the bead out the other side of the hopper. Slap it onto the corner,

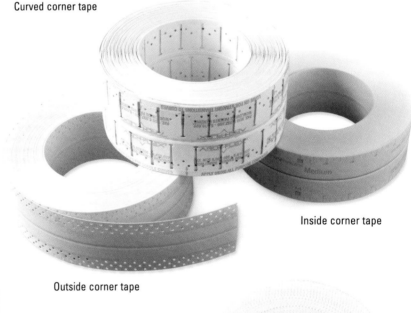

Curved corner tape

Inside corner tape

Outside corner tape

Flexible paper tape

Fiberglass mesh tape

and push firmly to seat it. A special corner roller makes that an easy job. Use a drywall knife to wipe up compound that squeezes out, and apply it as the first coat on the face of the tape.

Specialized bead designs allow you to create bullnose inside and outside corners—both straight and curved. Metal transition pieces convert from bullnose to square at corners to permit easier installation of crown molding, baseboards, and other millwork.

When you need to turn an outside bullnose corner, consider metal or plastic caps that permit construction of two- and three-way bullnose corners. See *page 101* for installation details.

J- and L-beads conceal the edge of a drywall panel when it butts against another material or is exposed. A metal or plastic control joint is used between the edges of drywall sheets to permit expansion and contraction that could otherwise deform or crack the panels. You may need to install a control joint in long runs of drywall, from the top of a door header to the ceiling, or across large ceiling expanses. A tape strip protects the expansion channel while you embed it into the compound. Zip off the strip when installation is complete.

## Repair patches

Repair patches streamline the tedious task of fitting scrap drywall to fill holes.

Perforated aluminum patches have a self-adhesive backing that makes installation a snap. You then simply top the patch with several layers of compound to make its edges disappear. Don't exceed the maximum hole size stated by the manufacturer, or you could risk creating a springy surface that flexes like the bottom of an old-fashioned oil can.

Composite patches are also perforated, but you need to "butter" the back with drywall compound to embed it. You'll find a variety of precut shapes that help you fix miscut openings for electrical boxes or ceiling fixtures. The precut shapes also allow you to cut your own custom shapes with a utility knife or scissors.

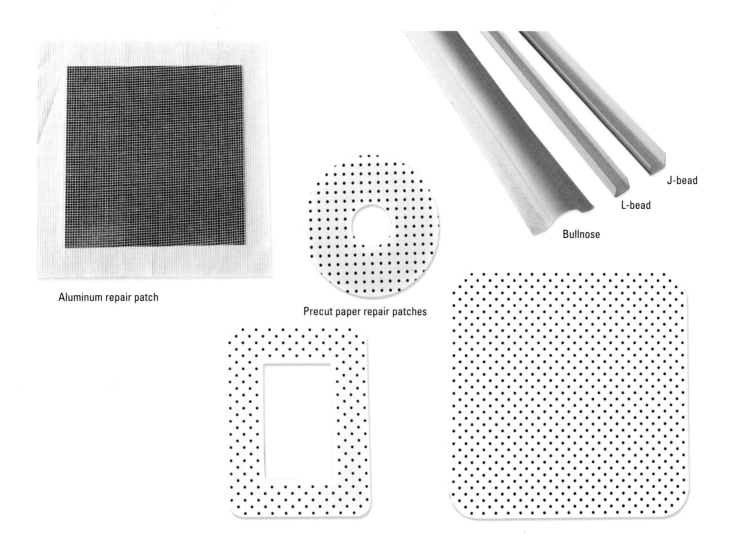

Aluminum repair patch

Precut paper repair patches

Bullnose

L-bead

J-bead

# DRYWALL COMPOUNDS

**D**rywall compounds, commonly called "mud" in the trade, come in such an astonishing variety that it could easily confuse a beginner. To discover the relative merits and shortcomings of each type, please refer to the detailed discussion in "Taping, Joint Compounds, & Sanding," *page 88.* Here's a quick rundown:

You'll sometimes see drywall joint compounds named for the function they perform. But excelling at that one purpose often means a compromise of other characteristics. For example, a taping compound is usually a setting-type that achieves high strength but is extremely difficult to sand. As a result, you'll want to make certain that subsequent coats will completely bury it.

Professionals know that compounds that are easy to sand, such as a topping compound, also have a texture that spreads more easily. But topping formulations, whether ready-mixed or setting type, lack the

Premixed topping compound

Setting-type joint compound

Setting-type lightweight joint compound

Premixed lightweight all-purpose compound

ngth for taped joints. Save the topping
mpound for the final coat.

l-purpose compounds represent a
npromise between strength and easy
ding. If you use one of these formulas,
'll sacrifice a bit of strength in the first
t and some ease of handling and

smoothing in later coats.

Setting-type and ready-mixed joint compounds produce similar results but achieve them in different ways. A setting-type compound is a powder that you add to water. The addition of moisture begins an irreversible chemical reaction that causes the ingredients to harden.

Ready-mixed joint compound hardens as the water in it evaporates.

If you can buy only one type of mud for your project, premixed all-purpose compound produces good results.For repairs, choose a nonshrinking surfacing compound or purchase drywall compound in a tube.

Premixed all-purpose compound

Setting-type spackling compound

Premixed all-purpose compound

Premixed all-purpose compound

Setting-type lightweight joint compound

Premixed lightweight all-purpose compound

# TOOLS

If a visit to the home center or hardware store makes you feel like a sweet-toothed kid in a candy store, you may be showing signs of becoming a tool addict. Keep a firm grip on the shopping cart, eyes straight ahead, and follow these pointers to help you buy the best tools without draining your bank account.

Even when you stumble across incredible deals, fight the urge to become a tool collector. Don't put that "I've always wanted" tool into your shopping cart until you absolutely need it for a project. A tool purchased because you think you might need it someday is destined to collect dust for years.

Follow this rule: When you do need a tool, purchase the best quality you can afford. This rule is especially important for drywall knives. At first glance, you may not be able tell much difference between a top-quality drywall knife and its lookalike cousin from the bargain bin. But the resiliency of the tool's steel is critical to achieving a smooth application of drywall compound. With the right tools, you'll get better results with reduced effort and in less time.

## Specialized and not-so-specialized tools

On the following pages, you'll discover that the drywall trade has some specialized equipment. Fortunately, most of the hand tools—even those that are top quality—are reasonably priced. And even more fortunately, you'll find that you can easily rent high-dollar items like a drywall lift at a sensible price from a local rental yard. Check the prices at several companies to find the best price.

As you gather the tools for your project, you'll find that you probably already have a number of them on hand. A chalk line and utility knife, for example, are toolbox "must-haves," but don't forget to check your inventory of powdered marking chalk and replacement knife blades before you begin your project. Squinting at faint lines or trying to make do with a dull blade will slow down your progress and can lead to mistakes. Gypsum drywall is very abrasive, and it quickly blunts cutting edges. Change the blade at the first sign of dullness.

## You'll work faster and achieve better results with quality, proper tools.

### CHAPTER PREVIEW

**Measuring and marking tools**
*page 30*

**Cutting and shaping tools**
*page 32*

**Support tools**
*page 34*

**Attachment tools**
*page 35*

*You probably already own many of the tools you'll need for a drywall project. The additional, specialized tools are not expensive. Purchase the best quality hand tools you can afford—they pay off in the long run.*

**Taping tools**
*page 36*

**Sanding tools**
*page 38*

**Texturing tools**
*page 40*

**Safety equipment**
*page 41*

# MEASURING AND MARKING TOOLS

This category includes some tools that have been in builders' tool kits for thousands of years. But you'll also find the latest stud-sensing technology—it's the next best thing to seeing into a wall. Equip yourself with a **tape measure,** pencils, a **mason's line,** a **plumb bob,** and a line level that clips onto a tightly stretched string. Choose a brightly colored line level so that it won't get lost amid construction debris. You'll need a **4-foot level** to check framing and as a dependable straightedge. Use a **chalk line** to mark long straight cutlines. It can also serve as a plumb bob. For drywall projects steer away from red chalk because it's a permanent color. Blue, the standard color, works well. You'll want squares in an assortment of sizes. A 12-inch **combination square** allows you to draw square lines, and it is handy for making layout lines at a specific distance in from the edge of a board. A drywall **T-square** is handy for laying

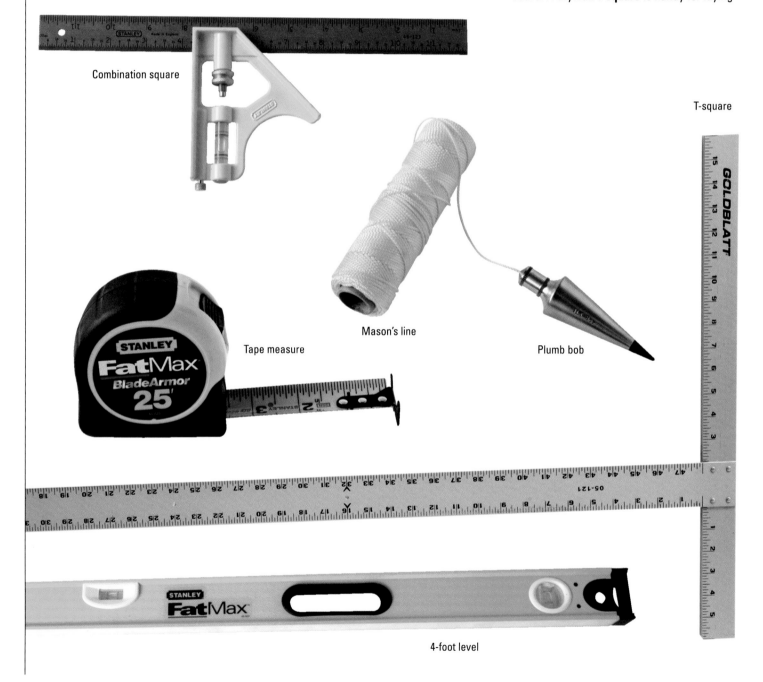

Combination square

T-square

Mason's line

Tape measure

Plumb bob

4-foot level

out and guiding cuts on a sheet of drywall. A **compass/scribe** helps mark circles and the contours of irregular surfaces. A **stud sensor** is used to find framing studs behind walls. Electronic and magnetic finders detect the nails in a wall. New models use sound to sense the density of the studs.

They can also help locate pipes and wiring inside a wall. A **water level** makes it easy to find and mark level on surfaces that are too far apart to use a carpenter's level—across a room, for example.

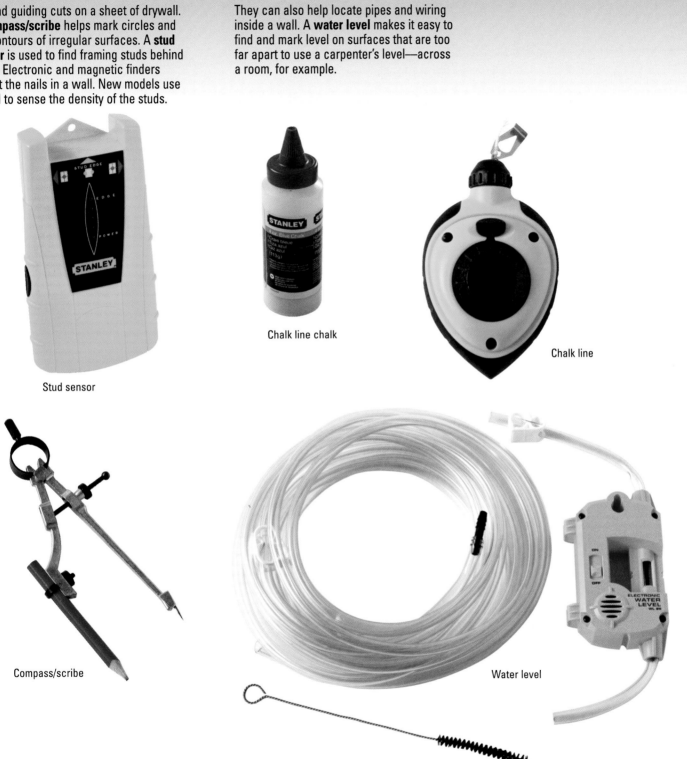

Stud sensor

Chalk line chalk

Chalk line

Compass/scribe

Water level

# CUTTING AND SHAPING TOOLS

**A** **utility knife** may be a basic tool, but it appears in an astonishing number of shapes. The fixed-blade knife is simple and dependable, but it demands a leather belt sheath or a dedicated slot in your tool belt. Retractable knives are versatile, and some feature ergonomic design refinements. But no matter what style of knife you choose, stockpile plenty of sharp blades, and change them at the first sign of dullness.

A **jab saw** is absolutely essential for making cutouts in drywall, and the basic model cuts on the push stroke. A more aggressive tooth pattern cuts on both the pull and push strokes, producing a faster but sometimes fuzzier cut. If the blade has specially hardened teeth, you can cut cementious backerboard. A larger drywall saw is also handy for cutting sheets at doorways and windows.

A **Surform®** **plane** is handy for trimming, such as when you want to plane an edge slightly to fit a corner.

Some drywall projects call for cutting a number of narrow pieces, and a strip cutter lets you mass-produce them in hurry. When it comes to cutting circles, you can mark

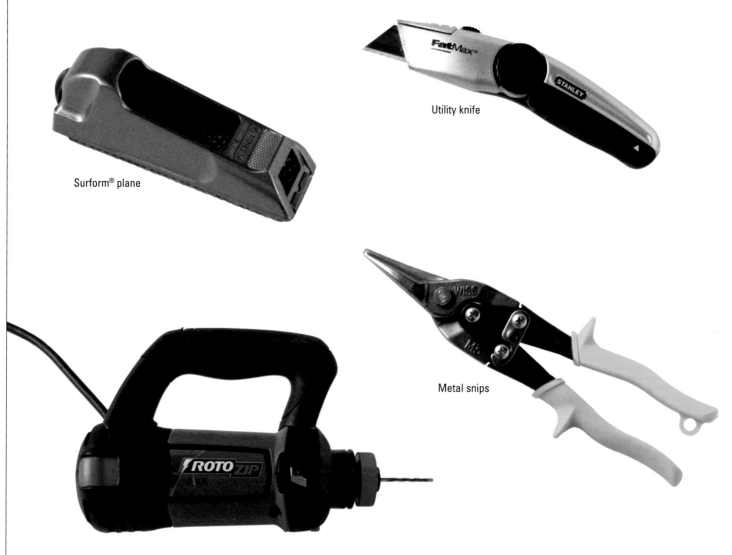

Utility knife

Surform® plane

Metal snips

Drywall router

and score drywall in a single step with an adjustable **circle cutter.** You'll find **hole saws** in a wide range of sizes to match common recessed ceiling fixtures.

A rasp with a replaceable blade refines cutlines and smoothes drywall edges. For the same function with cementious backerboard, you'll need an angle grinder with an **abrasive wheel** or diamond blade.

A circular saw with a carbide blade quickly cuts wood studs and other framing lumber. For cutting metal studs, put an abrasive wheel in your circular saw or opt for quieter cutting by slicing with compound-action **metal snips.**

A **drywall router** is the pro's choice to make cutouts for outlet boxes and other utilities. Add an accessory vacuum attachment, and you'll control dust right at the source. Use a special filter bag on a shop vac to deal with the fine dust created by drywall work.

Jab/drywall saw

Abrasive cutting wheel attachment for router

Hole saw

Circle cutter

# SUPPORT TOOLS

**W**ith a pair of **panel carriers** and a co-worker, move drywall sheets with confidence. Consider renting scaffolding if you're working in a room with soaring ceilings. Otherwise, an ordinary **stepladder** will be fine. A **panel lifter** is an item that's definitely worth renting if you're drywalling a ceiling. A deadman T-brace is a ceiling panel support that you make yourself (see *page 78*), and a clamping pole is a commercial alternative. Keep tools and fasteners within easy reach in a **tool belt**.

A **roll lifter** elevates wall panels up to a few inches and is especially handy when you hang the lower horizontal panel on a wall. If you don't want to invest in a dedicated tool for this function, use a flat **pry bar** with a scrap of lumber.

Tool belt

Panel Lifter

Ladders

Panel carrier

Pry bar

Roll lifter

# ATTACHMENT TOOLS

**A** drywall hammer has a domed face that's less likely to break the face paper of panels than a carpenter's hammer. The checkered pattern on the face also creates a slight texture that helps drywall compound adhere. The head is lighter and slightly larger than a standard hammer, and aligned at a slight angle, all to make it easier to set a nail properly into drywall. A nail slot helps you pull errant fasteners, and the end is tapered (but not sharpened) for prying tasks.

You'll need a **caulking gun** for applying panel adhesive. If you have to install a few plastic corner beads, buy a manual **staple gun.** If you're tackling a big project, consider renting or buying an electric or pneumatic (air-powered) gun.

Add a dimpler attachment to your drill, and you'll drive drywall screws with minimal risk of overdriving that breaks the face paper. A corded **screwgun** is an efficient driving tool that features a depth-limiting adjustment. Equip your screwgun with an accessory **self-feeding attachment,** and you'll drive fasteners that are collated on plastic strips. You can also purchase self-feeding screwguns that are corded or cordless.

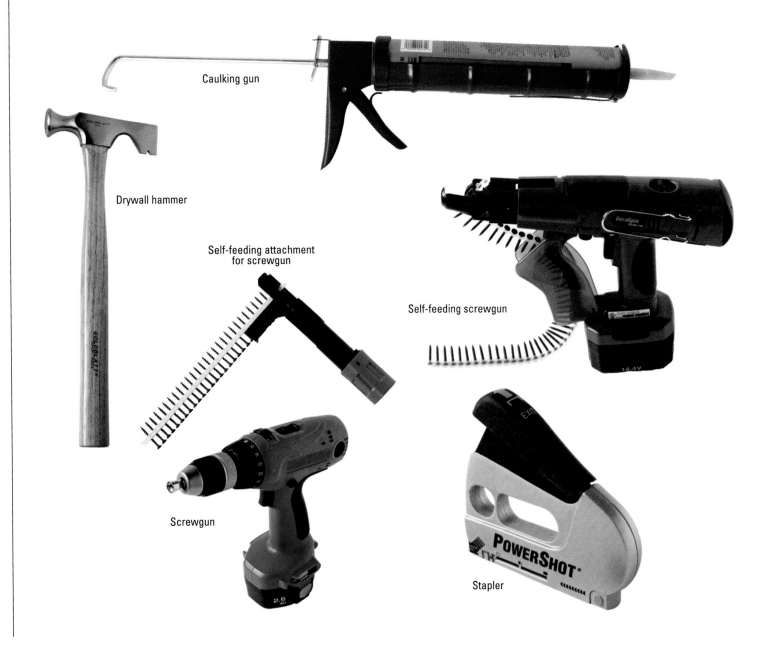

Caulking gun

Drywall hammer

Self-feeding attachment for screwgun

Self-feeding screwgun

Screwgun

Stapler

# TAPING TOOLS

**T**ools for spreading joint compound fall into two general categories: **trowels,** which look like concrete-smoothing tools with a handle parallel to the blade, and **knives,** which have a handle at a right angle to the blade. A curved blade drywall trowel slightly crowns the compound, a helpful feature when you're concealing butt joints. But for the majority of other applications, most people find that knives are more versatile and easier to handle. A basic set consists of three knives with blades that are 4 or 6 inches, 8 or 10 inches, and 12 or 14 inches. Plastic is the least expensive blade material, but most pros don't use them for anything but scooping compound out of a bucket. Blued steel is widely used, but stainless steel is much more rust resistant. Top-of-the-line drywall tools sometimes have cushioned grips that make them more comfortable to use.

Some people like inside and outside **corner tools,** feeling that they speed up the work. But others find them difficult to control and opt for working each side of the corner separately with a straight knife. You'll even find an adjustable-angle inside tool that adapts to a wide range of off angles.

If you're using ready-mixed drywall compound, buy a **hand mudmasher** to make sure that moisture is evenly distributed throughout the bucket. For mixing setting-

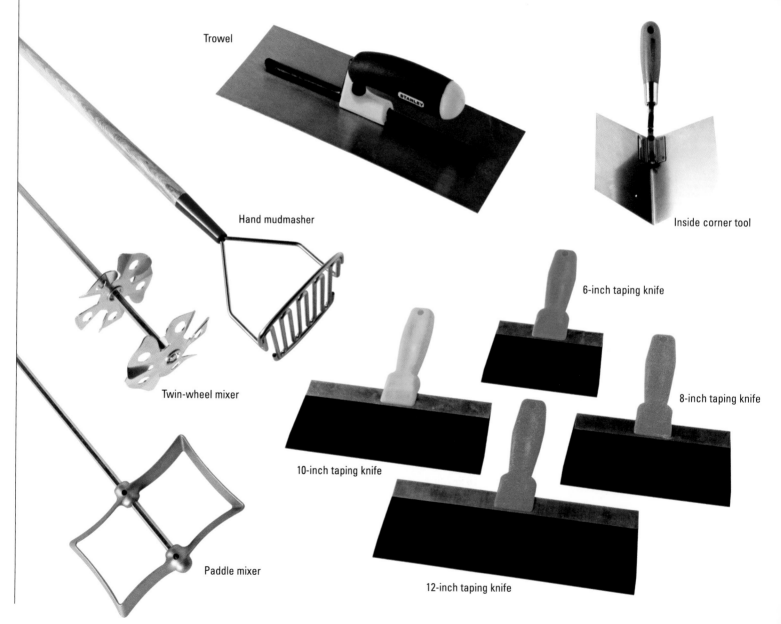

Trowel

Hand mudmasher

Inside corner tool

6-inch taping knife

Twin-wheel mixer

8-inch taping knife

10-inch taping knife

Paddle mixer

12-inch taping knife

type compound, you'll need a ½-inch variable-speed drill and a **mixer.** Professionals may discuss the fine points of the various mixer designs, but virtually any style will meet the requirements of the do-it-yourself worker.

If you apply paper drywall tape, consider a belt-hung **dispenser.** Some have a built-in folder that helps you tape inside corners faster. A mesh tape dispenser is like a tape gun with a trigger-activated cutter; it also has a flip-down roller for inside corners. If you work with composite tapes, consider a metal folder to save your fingers from abrasion. The **Banjo® taper** holds paper drywall tape in one compartment and joint compound in the other. The tool applies compound to the tape, speeding the embedding process on big jobs. On small jobs, however, the time required to clean the tool can outweigh the time saved.

Some people like to hold joint compound on a hawk (especially when working with a trowel), but a **mud pan** is generally a more popular choice. Plastic trays are inexpensive, but cleaning the removable metal strip can be an annoyance. Trays with angular corners are tougher to clean than round-bottom models. The most common mud pan length handles up to 12-inch knives. Look for the longer pan if you buy a 14-inch drywall knife.

Outside corner tool

Banjo® taper

12-inch plastic mud pan

14-inch mud pan

Joint tape dispenser

# SANDING TOOLS

**A**lthough your hardware store may have full sheets of **drywall sanding screen,** you'll find that die-cut strips load quickly into pole-mounted and hand sanders. Avoid ordinary sandpaper—it clogs too quickly. For conventional drywall compound, sand with -grit or finer abrasive; when you're sanding lightweight or topping compounds, choose 150-grit or finer.

The **swivel-joint pole sander** improves your reach and leverage whether you're sanding a ceiling or a wall. If you use 1- or 2-inch beads on outside corners, consider a corner bead cleaner. It mounts onto a standard handle to quickly remove unwanted joint compound.

A **cellulose sponge** can eliminate some dust during the sanding process. The sponge smoothes joints by slightly dissolving nonsetting-type joint compound. Consider the sponge a final smoothing

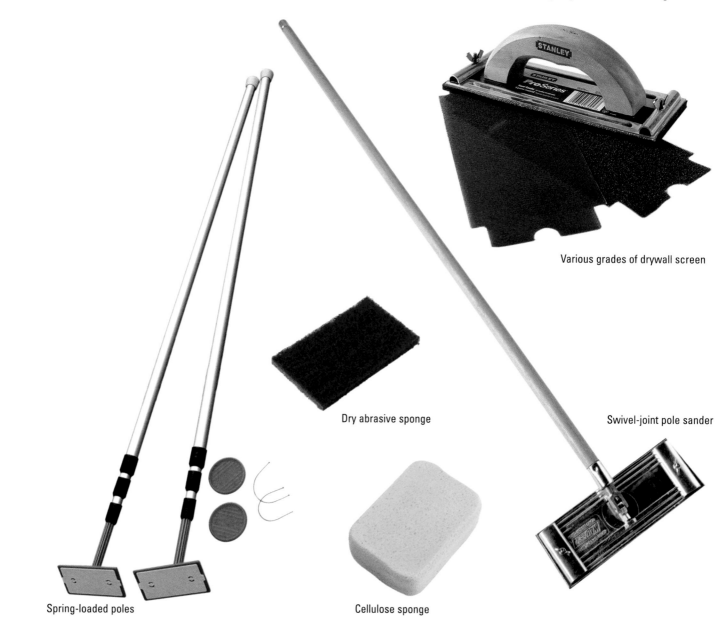

Various grades of drywall screen

Dry abrasive sponge

Swivel-joint pole sander

Spring-loaded poles

Cellulose sponge

step—not as a substitute for dry sanding. For actually sanding down compound, you can use a **dry abrasive sponge** or pad.

Contain sanding dust by raising walls of plastic sheeting held by adjustable **spring-loaded poles.** Setup is surprisingly quick, and it's a particularly good solution for remodeling projects. You can buy a basic system or fully accessorize it—including adhesive-backed zippers that make doors in the plastic and foam rails that dust-proof the edges.

For dust control right at the source, consider a sanding system that attaches to a shop vacuum. Some designs connect directly to the vacuum, while others utilize a **water filter** to grab the dust before it even gets to the vacuum.

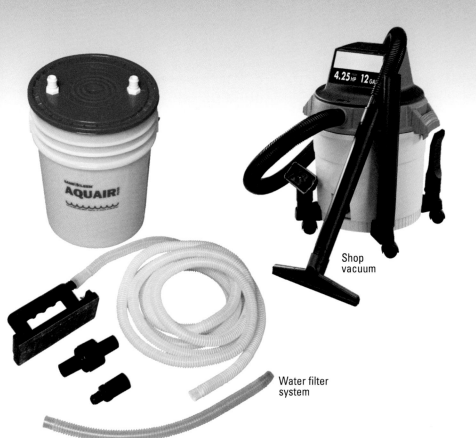

Shop vacuum

Water filter system

## Create a doorway

You won't need a full wall of sheeting if you are working in a room that is separated from the rest of the house by a door. There you can simply attach plastic sheeting over the doorway as a seal. However, you will still need to create a doorway in the plastic to gain access to the work area. Just cut the sheet by the door opening.

**1** When you put up the plastic, leave a fold of about 12–18 inches where the doorway will be. After the plastic is up, slit the sheet vertically to make two flaps.

**2** To seal the flaps, fold them together and clip them with two or three spring clamps.

# TEXTURING TOOLS

If you want to apply texture to walls or ceilings, you'll find a wide range of mechanical and manual tools. Home centers usually have a variety of **brushes** in the drywall section, but you can also explore the cleaning supply aisle for more choices.

You'll need a **hopper gun** to shoot "popcorn" texture onto ceilings. This gun also will spray thinned drywall compound onto walls and ceilings. A commercial-quality airless sprayer also will apply thinned compound, and its gun is lighter and easier to handle. Although ceiling glitter is currently out of style, you can purchase the shiny particles and a manual applicator gun.

Knock down sprayed texture with a wide drywall knife. A broad **wipedown blade**—24 inches or wider—scrapes oversprayed texture material from unmasked walls after you shoot the ceiling.

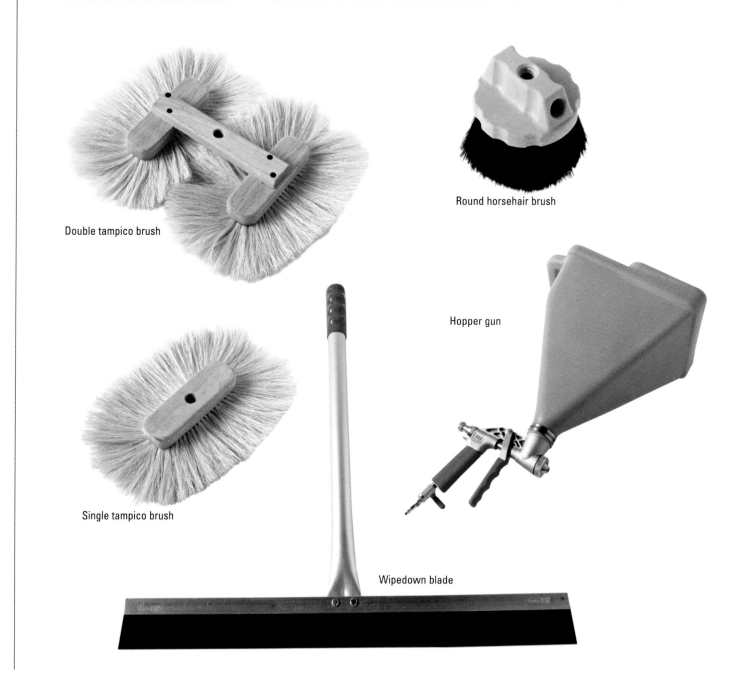

Double tampico brush

Round horsehair brush

Single tampico brush

Hopper gun

Wipedown blade

# SAFETY EQUIPMENT

**S**afety glasses or goggles are a must when you're doing any construction work. When you choose a **dust mask,** look for one with a NIOSH 95 rating to capture fine dust. If the mask has an exhalation valve, you'll literally breathe easier.

A painter's cap protects your head when you're sanding, but you may want to put on a **hardhat** when installing ceiling panels. Glue a sponge on top of the hardhat and use your head to hold the drywall in position without marring it. A back support brace encourages proper lifting posture. Use **hearing protection** when working with power tools.

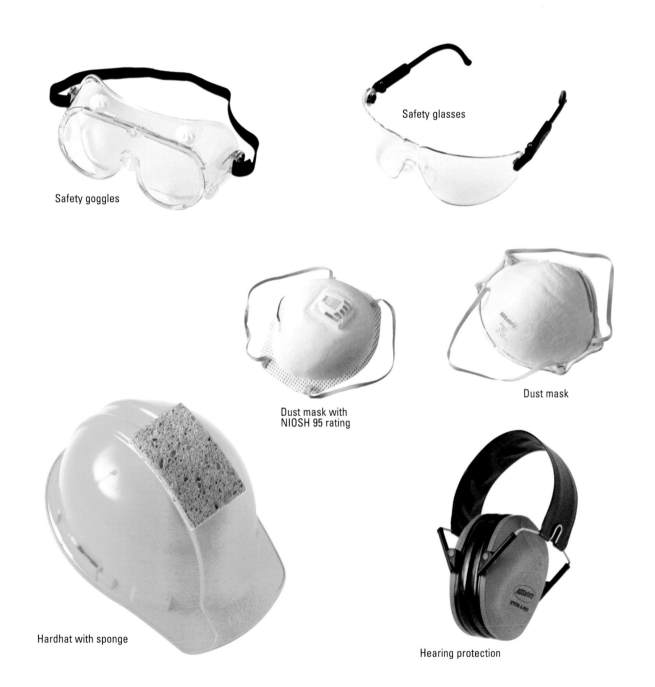

Safety goggles

Safety glasses

Dust mask with
NIOSH 95 rating

Dust mask

Hardhat with sponge

Hearing protection

# FRAMING FOR DRYWALL

In the construction industry, two different trades cooperate in wall construction: the rough-in carpenters set the framing and the drywall crew hangs and finishes the panels. But when you're handling the details of both trades in a remodeling project, working carefully as a framer makes your job easier when you switch to your drywalling role.

This chapter reveals ways to check your work to ensure that the walls are flat and doorway openings are plumb and aligned. You'll also discover how to correct a wavy ceiling, adding furring strips so that your new ceiling is smooth and flat.

## Wood and metal framing

Wood is the traditional choice for wall framing, but check out the advantages of metal framing for your next remodeling project. If you're converting an attic into extra living area, you can simply tuck a bundle of ten metal studs under your arm, and walk up the stairs. If you're making a basement or garage recreation room, metal studs eliminate a food source for termites, ants, and other insects. And there's no tedious lumber-sorting in the quest for straight studs. Metal studs start straight and stay that way.

## Concrete fasteners

Some do-it-yourselfers figure that it will be easy to anchor into the concrete of their 30-year-old house. But surprisingly, concrete usually gets stronger with age, slowly but surely getting harder for decades. Although there's a bewildering variety of concrete fasteners on the market, we've sorted them and provided installation tips so you can choose the style that's right for your project.

## Special projects

Architectural features can separate your home from the ordinary. Consider a sweeping curved wall, a barrel-vaulted ceiling, or an archway. A soffit above new kitchen cabinets can be decorative, or it can conceal runs of heat ducts, plumbing pipes, and electrical wires.

**If the framing is straight and square, the rest of the job will move ahead with ease.**

## CHAPTER PREVIEW

**Framing a wall with wood studs**
*page 44*

**Framing a wall with metal studs**
*page 46*

**Fastening to concrete**
*page 50*

**Building a soffit**
*page 52*

Like the foundation of a house, the framing or other surface under drywall is crucial not only to its looks but also to its strength. Preparation up front helps prevent frustration and flaws later.

**Framing a curved wall**
*page 54*

**Making a wavy ceiling flat**
*page 56*

**Creating sound control and firewalls**
*page 58*

**Checking and correcting framing**
*page 60*

# FRAMING A WALL WITH WOOD STUDS

**W**hen you add a wall in your house, it will either run perpendicular or parallel to the ceilings joists. Perpendicular construction is easier because you have built-in attachment points for the top plate where it crosses each joist. Parallel construction involves a bit more work because you'll need to add blocking between the joists. Shifting the wall so it's directly under a joist eliminates the blocking, but make sure you can live with that location instead of choosing it simply to save some work.

Building the wall on the floor is the most efficient procedure, but space limitations may sometimes force you to build the wall in place. To do that, plumb the top and bottom plates to each other, and fasten the studs to the plates by toenailing (driving fasteners at an angle).

## PRESTART CHECKLIST

☐ **TIME**
If you have a helper, allow at least one hour for a simple 8-foot-long wall that runs perpendicular to the joists. Framing openings such as doorways or windows will add time to the project.

☐ **TOOLS**
Tape measure, stud finder, chalk line, plumb bob with nylon line, hammer or power screwdriver, level, circular saw

☐ **SKILLS**
Measuring; snapping a chalk line; crosscutting; driving fasteners; using a stud finder, plumb bob, level

☐ **PREP**
Draw project plans and locate joists

☐ **MATERIALS**
2×4 studs, 2×4 top and bottom plates, 16d (3½-inch) nails or 3½-inch screws, tapered shims

**1** With a helper, hold the top plate in place along the chalk line and nail it in place right through the ceiling. If the plate isn't quite straight, nail part of it, then push the offending end into line.

**2** Place the studs on edge in between the plates. If any studs are not perfectly flat, turn them so that any slight gap is at the bottom. Hold them in position one by one and nail them in place through the plates. Make sure the edges of the studs are flush with the edges of the plates.

### Running a wall parallel to the joists

**1** Use a handsaw or reciprocating saw to cut away the ceiling flush to the inside faces of the joists where the wall will attach. (For cutting a plaster ceiling, see *page 134.*) Snap a chalk line along the center of each joist, then use a utility knife to cut away a ¾-inch-wide strip of drywall. This exposes a surface on the joist onto which you can attach the new drywall.

**2** Nail the blocking in place between the joists. Space the pieces 16 inches on center to provide support for the new drywall.

**3** Dangle a plumb bob from the end and side of the ceiling plate to transfer the wall location to the floor. If you are working alone, hang the plumb bob from a nail in the plate. Repeat at the other end. This job is quicker with two people: One holds the string, the other marks the spot.

—Plumb bob

**4** Anchor the wall by nailing up through the top plate into the ceiling plate. Make sure the edges of the two plates are flush. To protect a plaster ceiling, install the plate with 2½-inch-long drywall screws. Check the wall for plumb with a carpenter's level, then nail the bottom plate to the floor.

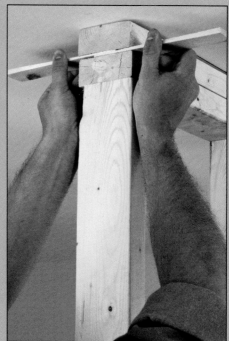

**5** If there is a little space between the top plate and the ceiling plate, slip a pair of shims in between the two before nailing. Drive the nails through the shims to keep them from slipping out.

## FRAMING AND DRYWALL REQUIREMENTS FOR BUILDING WALLS AND CEILINGS

| Thickness of panel | Location | Application direction (1) | Maximum frame spacing o.c. (on center) |
|---|---|---|---|
| **Single layer ⅜ in.** | Ceilings (2) | Perpendicular or parallel | 16 in. |
| **Single layer ½ in.** | Ceilings | Perpendicular | 24 in. (3) (4) |
| | | Parallel | 16 in. |
| | Walls | Perpendicular or parallel | 24 in. |
| | | Parallel (5) | 16 in. |
| **Single layer ⅝ in.** | Ceilings (4) | Perpendicular | 24 in. |
| | Walls | Perpendicular or parallel | 24 in. |
| **Double layer ⅜ in.** | Ceilings (6) | Perpendicular | 16 in. |
| | Walls | Perpendicular or parallel | 24 in. (7) |
| **Double layer ½ or ⅝ in.** | Ceilings | Perpendicular or parallel | 24 in. (7) |
| | Walls | Perpendicular or parallel | 24 in. |

*(1) Application direction refers to the position of the long edge of the drywall panel relative to the framing. (2) Not recommended below unheated spaces such as an attic. (3) Maximum spacing is 16 inches if water-based texturing material is applied. (4) If special ceiling board is utilized, maximum spacing for perpendicular application is 24 in. o.c. if weight of unsupported insulation does not exceed 1.3 pounds per square foot (psf); with spacing at 16 in. o.c., weight of unsupported insulation should not exceed 2.2 psf. (5) Not recommended if water-based texturing material is applied. (6) Use adhesive to laminate ⅜-inch panel in double-layer construction. (7) Spacing of 16 inches o.c. is usually required for fire-rated construction.*

# FRAMING A WALL WITH METAL STUDS

**M**etal studs have a lot to recommend them to a homeowner who's considering a remodeling project. Metal studs are straight when you buy them, and stay that way. They don't burn, rust, or rot, and termites and other insects can't eat them. They don't burn like wood, and are lightweight and easy to cut and fasten. The factory-punched holes eliminate drilling for the installation of wiring and plumbing, which speeds along those tasks.

Most walls in remodeling projects are nonloadbearing, meaning that they don't help support the weight of the house. If you need to build a loadbearing wall, make sure that your metal studs are rated for that use.

If you're accustomed to working with wood construction, metal studs may initially seem flimsy. That's because they're not designed for strength on their own—instead, they partner with the drywall as a systems approach to wall construction.

## PRESTART CHECKLIST

☐ **TIME**
When working with a helper, allow at least one hour for a simple 8-foot-long wall that runs perpendicular the joists. Framing openings such as doorways or windows will add time to the project.

☐ **TOOLS**
Gloves, metal snips, chalk line, plumb bob with nylon line, tape measure, level, stud finder (if joists are concealed), power screwdriver, C-clamp self-locking pliers

☐ **SKILLS**
Measuring; snapping a chalk line; cutting metal; driving fasteners; using a stud finder, plumb bob, and level

☐ **PREP**
Draw project plans and locate joists

☐ **MATERIALS**
Metal studs and channel, fasteners to attach channels to floor and joists, assembly screws

**1** On the floor, lay out the position of the wall, and snap chalk lines to mark the wall's edges. Cut the runner at the edge of door openings. Attach the runner to the floor, using wood screws when working on a plywood surface. (Panhead or flathead screws provide the best holding power.) Fasten to concrete with powder-actuated fasteners, concrete screws, or screws driven into expansion plugs. For more information on fastening to concrete, see *page 50.* For long runs, see "Splicing a Runner," *page 47.*

**2** Transfer the location of the runner to the ceiling by twisting a stud into the floor runner and holding a level against it. Mark the stud's edges on the ceiling at each end of the wall, and join the marks by snapping a chalk line.

## Steel framing terminology

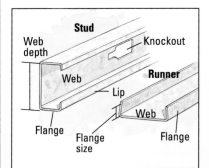

You'll find steel studs and runners in sizes that are similar to wood. For example, a nominal steel 2×4 has a web depth of 3.5 inches, and a steel 2×6 has a 5½-inch web. The minimum flange size is 1⅝ inch, and the maximum is 2 inches. The lip on steel studs improves their rigidity. The flanges of the track usually toe in slightly so they firmly grip the flanges of the studs.

## MAXIMUM NONLOADBEARING WALL HEIGHTS WITH SELECTED STUD SIZES

| Nominal size and designation (mils) [1] | Industry designator | Stud sizes | |
| --- | --- | --- | --- |
| | | 16 in. O.C. [2] | 24 in. O.C. * |
| 2 x 4 - 18 | 350S125-18 | 9' 10" | 6' 6" [3] |
| 2 x 4 - 27 | 350S125-27 | 15' 10" | 13' 10" |
| 2 x 4 - 33 | 350S125-33 | 17' 0" | 14' 10" |

*(1) The industry is moving away from gauge numbers as a thickness designation and toward mils. One mil is one-thousandth of an inch, and refers to the minimum thickness of the steel stock before corrosion protection is applied. For reference, 18 mils = 25 gauge; 27 mils = 22 gauge; 33 mils = 20 gauge.*

*(2) O.C. = on center*

*(3) Note that these studs are not suitable for standard 8-foot walls when spaced 24 inches o.c.*

**3** Attach the runner to the ceiling by driving screws into the joists. If the wall runs parallel to the joists, add blocking as shown on *page 113* for a wood wall. If you attach ceiling drywall to the underside of a roof truss system, professionals recommend a special resilient channel design that accommodates the potential movement of the truss. Check with your steel-framing supplier for more information.

**4** Lay out the stud locations on the edge of the bottom runner, using a permanent marker and a length of wood that equals the stud spacing. Although you could mark the centerline of the studs, you'll probably find it less confusing to mark one edge, then mark a quick X where the stud goes. You don't need to mark the upper runner. Double-check the spacing of the layout before you attach any studs.

**5** Cut the studs to length if necessary. Insert a stud into the upper and lower track with a twisting motion. Make certain that the open side of all studs faces the same direction. Align the edge of the stud with the mark on the floor runner, and clamp it with C-clamp self-locking pliers designed for welders. Drive a screw to secure the stud to the runner.

## Splicing a runner

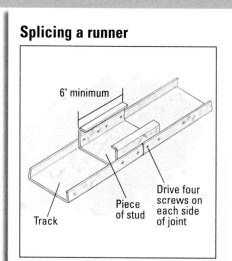

6" minimum

Drive four screws on each side of joint

Piece of stud

Track

Join lengths of track by using the simple method shown in the drawing. Make sure that the splice doesn't land at a stud location, and offset joints in the upper and lower tracks by at least 12 inches for maximum wall strength.

## Cut the studs to length

Compound-leverage aviation snips are usually the most practical method of cutting metal tracks and studs. These snips usually have handles (or another part) that are color coded. Red is for left cuts (most useful for right-handed people), green is for right cuts (usually preferred by left-handers), and yellow is for straight cuts *(page 32)*.

If you can't afford all three, buy the yellow plus the color that matches your working-hand preference. Slice through both flanges, then cut the web.

## The ideal screw

To join steel studs to the track, you need a self-drilling screw that creates a pilot hole through both pieces before the threads engage. You also want a head design that has a large diameter to spread the holding force. In addition, the head should have a very low profile so that it doesn't create a hump under the drywall. Last, you want a drive slot that's easy to use. The fastener that meets all of these specifications is a No. 8×½-inch modified truss head self-drilling screw with phillips drive. You'll find these screws (or a very similar design) where you buy your framing steel.

# Framing a wall with metal studs *(continued)*

**6** To make a header, cut a length of runner 4 inches longer than the opening. Draw a line square across the web 2 inches from one end, and another line square across at the opposite end to mark the length of the opening. Cut V-notches into the flanges, aiming at the lines on the web (see inset). Bend the runner along the lines and drive a screw through each tab and into the king stud.

**7** Create an attachment surface for wall cabinets by notching a length of runner and screwing it to the flanges of the studs. Consult your cabinet installer to make certain of the runner's height and to alert him that he'll need sheet metal screws for the installation.

**8** Add blocking of solid wood or plywood to simplify the installation of baseboards, crown moldings, shelves, and accessories like towel bars. This also is an alternative strategy to the previous step for hanging cabinets. With blocking, you can drive nails or screws just as you can with a wood-stud wall. Without wood backing, install moldings to the studs with construction adhesive and trimhead screws.

## WHAT IF...
### You want to install a door?

When you fasten wood door jambs or molding to steel framing, use trimhead screws. These fasteners have heads that are barely larger than a countersunk nail. Drive them about $1/32$ inch below the wood's surface and fill the hole with putty. Another strategy combines wood with metal framing. Line the opening with wood bucks as shown in the drawing, and you'll have a solid target for nailing. Substitute wood for the two full-length king studs that flank the opening to gain a broader nailing surface for the door's molding.

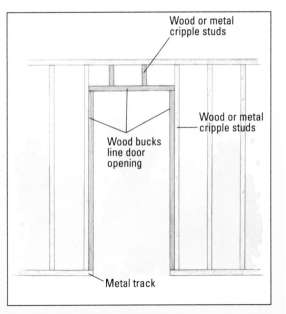

Wood or metal cripple studs

Wood or metal cripple studs

Wood bucks line door opening

Metal track

**STANLEY** PRO TIP

### Align the punchouts

When you install studs, make sure the punchouts align with each other to simplify the task of pulling wires or installing pipes.

**9** Snap plastic grommets into the knockouts to prevent the sharp edges of the stud from slicing the insulation on electrical wires. Alternatively, consider armored cable or conduit. The grommets prevent metal-to-metal contact with water piping—an electrolysis situation that can corrode both pipes and studs. If you can't find grommets, improvise with lengths of foam pipe insulation.

**10** Install the drywall by driving type S fine-threaded screws into the studs. For best results, drive the screws along one stud before moving to the next one. Always work toward the open C-shape of the studs, as detailed on *page 84*.

## Another way to fasten metal

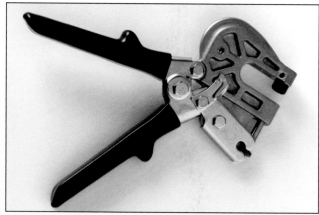

If you get into a big project, you may want to consider the advantages offered by a punch lock stud crimper. This tool uses compound leverage to create a rectangular crimp that mechanically locks the stud and track together, forming a strong bond. The tool is easy to maneuver into tight quarters, and you never need to worry about running out of screws.

## More ways to cut steel

Cutting steel with hand tools isn't difficult, but extended cutting sessions can be tough on a weekend remodeler. You can put power on your side by fitting your circular saw or miter saw with a steel-cutting abrasive blade. Cutting is quick and easy, but it's extremely noisy and can produce an impressive shower of sparks.

Be sure to wear eye and hearing protection, and help prevent a fire by cutting outdoors and making certain that sparks don't smolder on dust within the saw. A compound leverage channel shear is a possible rental item that multiplies your arm strength to slice through studs and channel without deforming the steel's profile.

# FASTENING TO CONCRETE

**W**hich type of fastener is right for you? For speed, it's impossible to beat powder-actuated fasteners. But unless you've already invested in this tool, you'll have to factor in the time involved in two round trips to the rental center and filling out the paperwork. If you're finishing an entire basement, you'll save enough time to make the rental process worthwhile. But it's a questionable call for installing a single wall.

No matter which fastener you choose, consider 1 inch of concrete penetration as the minimum. To increase holding power, choose a fastener that burrows deeper into the concrete or has a larger diameter. With the blue screws shown at right, for example, one with a diameter of $\frac{1}{4}$ inch has more than twice the pullout resistance of a $\frac{3}{16}$-inch screw when both are driven 1 inch deep into concrete. Driving the fasteners $1\frac{3}{4}$ deep more than triples the pullout resistance for the $\frac{3}{16}$-inch screw and the $\frac{1}{4}$-incher is nearly three times stronger. In shear (perpendicular to the long axis of the fastener), the $\frac{1}{4}$-inch screw is nearly twice as strong as the $\frac{3}{16}$-inch version.

**With steel track,** you can install a fastener as short as 20 mm, but a 27 mm length produces the better penetration and superior strength. Choose a 72-mm fastener length when working with 2× stock. The boosters (powder cartridges) are available in a variety of color-coded strengths to match the fastener to the density of your concrete. A yellow booster is about midway on the power range and is usually a good starting point.

**If the concrete is less than a year old**, you may be able to drive special hardened concrete nails. Some concrete nails are the cut-nail design, shown in the photo, with a thick flat shank and a tapering V-profile. Other nails have a thick shank that sometimes has spiral ridges for improved holding power. Choose a length that will penetrate the concrete at least 1 inch. Be sure to wear safety goggles when hammering masonry nails into concrete.

## PRESTART CHECKLIST

☐ **TIME**
The time varies widely—from a few seconds each for powder-driven fasteners to several minutes' drilling time for other fasteners.

☐ **TOOLS**
Wood bits and carbide-tipped concrete bits, drill, hammer, wrenches

☐ **SKILLS**
Drilling

☐ **PREP**
Lay out spacing of fasteners on sole plate: one fastener near each end of the wall, and one in every other stud bay

☐ **MATERIALS**
Your choice of fasteners

**STANLEY** PRO TIP

### Switch bits for faster drilling

A carbide-tipped bit is ideal for drilling concrete, and it does an acceptable job of punching through steel runner, but it drills poorly through wood. So it's a good idea to drill holes in the sole plate with an ordinary wood bit before you tip the wall into place. Then you can switch to your carbide bit, and use the holes through the wood to guide the carbide bit.

**Masonry screws are an easy solution** to concrete fastening chores *(page 23)*. When you buy the screws, you'll also need to get a special bit that makes a pilot hole matched to the fastener. Drill at least ¼ inch deeper into the concrete than the fastener's embedment, and suck dust out of the hole with a shop vac. The hex-head style has an integral washer to spread the bearing pressure for a firm grip.

**There are several different styles of drop-in anchors.** The style shown is called a sleeve anchor, and it installs easily through identical-sized holes in both the sole plate and concrete. Tightening the hex nut pulls on the bolt and expands the slotted metal sleeve within the hole.

**A hammer-drive anchor** requires only a small pilot hole—the one shown requires only a ¼-inch hole. Drill the hole at least ¼ inch deeper than the length of the lower portion, and vacuum or blow out the hole. Drop in the anchor, and hammer on the pin to expand the bottom of the shield against the wall of the hole.

## Adhesive boosts holding power

Construction adhesive offers additional strength when combined with mechanical fasteners, but don't rely on adhesive alone to anchor the wall. A single wavy bead of adhesive is adequate; dual strips spread over a larger area and produce a stronger bond.

## Lag shields—an old standby

Lag shields produce strong joints, but they involve more installation steps than most fasteners. Drill holes through the wood sole plate with a wood bit and mark the floor. Move the sole plate, drill the floor, suck out the dust, and tap the shield into place. Replace the sole plate and drive lag screws with washers into the shields.

# BUILDING A SOFFIT

A soffit (also called a bulkhead) is an architectural element that's often utilized to fill up the space between the top of wall-mounted cabinets and the ceiling. Although the space it encloses is mostly empty, it's a great place to run wiring, heat ducts, and other utilities. Over sinks, a soffit often houses a canister light.

Although it's possible to build a soffit with a depth that exactly matches that of your cabinets, that design route multiplies the degree of difficulty for the cabinet installer. In most cases, the soffit is considerably deeper than the cabinets. For example, making the soffit 1½ inches deeper than the cabinets disguises minor cabinet alignment discrepancies and also permits the installation of a small molding strip.

When you're designing your soffit, don't forget to allow for an overhang at the exposed ends of soffit runs. Also be sure to allow for the thickness of the drywall on the front and bottom. You don't need to over-engineer the soffit because it's not a structural feature.

Take care to build the soffit level and square—it will help simplify installation of the cabinets.

**1** Fasten 1×4s to the back sides of the upper and lower 2×2 runners with nails or screws, creating a ladder-like construction. Place a vertical support at each end and about 16 inches on center throughout. Make sure you keep the assembly straight, square, and flat.

**2** Snap a chalk line onto the bottom of the joists parallel to the wall. To run a soffit parallel to the joists, you'll probably have to add nailers between the joists as shown on *page 44*. If you're framing an L- or U-shape soffit, install the first part parallel to the longest wall, then square the other soffit legs to it.

## Turning a corner

Wall construction involves inside/outside corners as well as T-walls. The drawings present strategies for framing these junctions in both wood and steel.

If you choose the assembly shown in the T-wall drawing (near right), you'll notice that the blocking can be a full-length stud or you can substitute short pieces of stud material—a strategy that saves money and also helps scraps disappear. If you're attaching your new wall to an outside wall, insulate any cavities between the blocking before attaching the second wall.

The construction shown in T-wall (far right) is more economical in terms of materials, and you can insulate the cavity after you've completed the framing.

### Corner framing

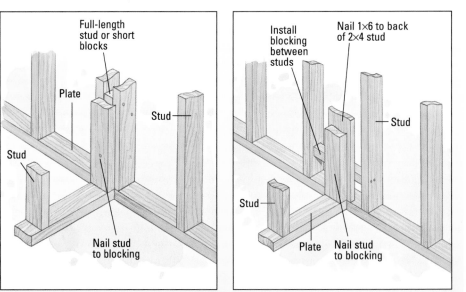

Full-length stud or short blocks

Plate

Stud

Stud

Nail stud to blocking

Install blocking between studs

Nail 1×6 to back of 2×4 stud

Stud

Stud

Plate

Nail stud to blocking

**3** Tack-nail the runner assembly to only two joists. Check for level along the length of the lower runner. Add tapered softwood shims, if necessary, between the upper runner and joist to level the assembly and to eliminate any gaps. If possible, drive your fastener through the shim to make sure it stays in place. Otherwise, smear a touch of woodworker's glue or construction adhesive on both sides of the shim near its tip to secure it to the framing. Let the glue dry before you trim the shims.

**4** Use a level to transfer the position of the bottom runner onto the wall studs. You need to mark only the ends, and then join the marks with a chalk line. Screw or nail the 2×2 wall runner to the studs.

**5** Screw 1×4 horizontal supports to the top edge of the wall runner and the lower runner. You can space these about 48 inches on center. Make sure the soffit stays square. Cover the face and bottom of the soffit with drywall. Install corner bead on outside corners *(page 101)* and tape the inside corners *(page 97)*.

## Framing a corner

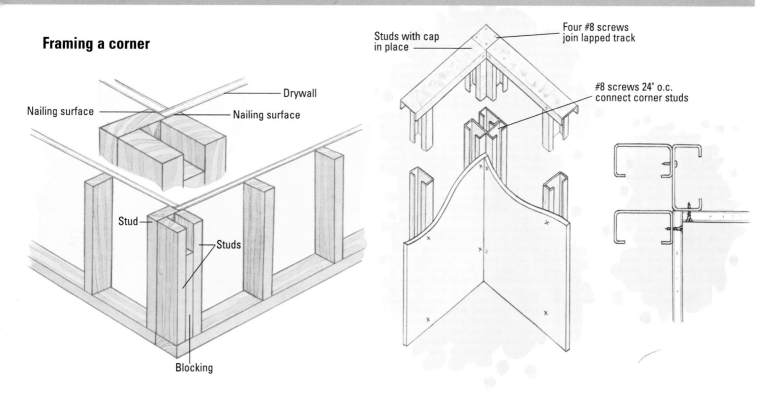

Drywall

Nailing surface

Nailing surface

Stud

Studs

Blocking

Studs with cap in place

Four #8 screws join lapped track

#8 screws 24" o.c. connect corner studs

# FRAMING A CURVED WALL

**A** curved wall can be a simple sweeping arc or an undulating wave that moves back and forth. Either way, a curved wall will add interest and drama to any room.

A flexible metal track speeds and simplifies the construction of the wall whether you utilize metal or wood studs. The track shown is also available in a model that accommodates 2×6 studs. Making your own curved track from standard channel is a bit tedious but not especially difficult. Making plates from solid wood or laminated plywood is another option, but it's a process that can consume significant amounts of both materials and time.

One of the key design considerations is the radius of the curves. Please see the chart on *page 110* for the minimum bending radii of a variety of panels. The radius you choose then determines the spacing of the studs. The chart shows the maximum stud spacing for a variety of radii. However, spacing the studs even more closely can give a smoother look to your finished wall.

Utilize these same construction techniques to make barrel vaults and wavy ceilings.

## PRESTART CHECKLIST

☐ **TIME**
Allow 20 minutes per lineal foot of wall

☐ **TOOLS**
Permanent marker, chalk line, plumb bob with nylon line, strip of scrap hardboard, drill/driver, drill bits, metal snips, masking tape, locking-grip pliers

☐ **SKILLS**
Measuring, using a plumb bob, driving fasteners

☐ **PREP**
Design the shape of the wall

☐ **MATERIALS**
Flexible track for the top and bottom of the wall, studs, fasteners

**1** Draw the curve on the floor with a permanent marker. To get a smooth curve, make a giant compass from a strip of hardboard or plywood. Tap a nail through the hardboard into the floor for the pivot point. Drill a hole at the other end at the desired radius for the curve; put the marker tip through the hole and draw.

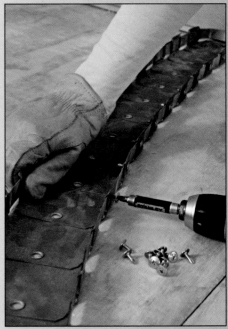

**2** Bend the track to shape, and hold the curve while you drive screws through the tabs into the metal strip. For best results, use No. 8×½-inch self-drilling screws. Driving a screw through every tab on both sides gives the strongest results (see *page 47*).

**STANLEY** PRO TIP

### Hold the curve

Run masking tape along the outside (convex) edge of the track to hold the curve while you drive screws into the inside (concave) edge. When you're ready to drive screws into the outside edge, you can pull the tape off or leave it in place and drill through it.

**3** After you've completed the first track, turn it over to use as a template to shape the top track. The top track is a mirror image of the bottom. Attach the second track to the first with locking-grip pliers at one end, shape the curve, then secure the other end with another pair of locking-grip pliers. Drive the screws.

**4** Attach the bottom track to the floor, and use a plumb bob to position the second track to the joists above you. Temporarily placing a few studs into the tracks means that the person on the ladder doesn't need to support the entire weight of the upper track. Check the alignment of the tracks at both ends and at the middle.

**5** Twist the studs into the tracks, and plumb them before driving screws through the track to secure them. You can use either wood or metal studs. For the smoothest wall surface, space the studs closely together, never exceeding the spacing recommended in the chart on *page 45*.

## Build an archway

Flexible track is an easy solution to the construction of archways. Simply bend mirror-image curves and join the tracks with short lengths of wood or metal studs.

## Make your own flexible track

To make your own flexible track, start with a length of steel runner. Cut through one flange and the web at 2-inch intervals along the portion that will be curved. Inside the runner, lay a steel strap that's at least 1 inch wide and with a thickness of at least 18 mils (25 gauge). Screw the flanges to the strip to set the curve. To make an S-shape curve, switch the cuts to the other flange of the runner.

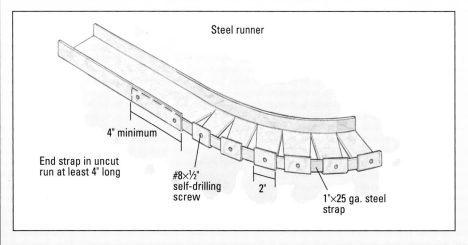

Steel runner

4" minimum

End strap in uncut run at least 4" long

#8×½" self-drilling screw

2"

1"×25 ga. steel strap

# MAKING A WAVY CEILING FLAT

Older homes—particularly those with plaster construction—may have cracked and wavy ceilings. If you install drywall directly to this surface, you'll still have a wavy ceiling minus the cracks. That's some improvement, but not enough to justify the effort.

The real solution involves the installation of furring strips—either wood as shown here or the resilient channels you'll read about on *page 58*. To get a ceiling that's flat, you need to find the lowest spot on the ceiling and shim all the furring to that point. It's not as difficult as it initially sounds. The procedure shown here is a systematic method for locating the lowest spot on a ceiling, then installing the furring strips.

You may need a good number of shims to complete the furring strip installation, but you can easily make them at home from scraps of plywood and hardboard.

## PRESTART CHECKLIST

☐ **TIME**
The time somewhat depends on the condition of the existing ceiling. For a room that measures 10×12 feet, you and your helper should allow at least 4 to 6 hours to check the ceiling and install the furring.

☐ **TOOLS**
Stud finder, hammer, ladders, two chalk lines with different colors of chalk, mason's line, level, line level

☐ **SKILLS**
Measuring and accurate marking, leveling, driving fasteners

☐ **PREP**
Clear the room, mark the location of all ceiling joists

☐ **MATERIALS**
Shims, furring strips, nails, screws for installing strips

**1** If the joists are hidden by drywall or plaster, use a stud finder to locate them, then snap chalk lines to indicate the centerline of each one. Using a different color chalk, mark the centerlines of the furring strips, typically 16 inches on center.

**2** Cut two 1×3 furring strips about 1 inch shorter than the two ends of the room that are at right angles to the joists. Drive nails every 12 inches along the top edges of the boards, leaving about ½ inch exposed. Tack-nail the first strip to one wall, leveling it with the top edge about ¾ inch below the ceiling.

## Making shims

For this project, flat shims work great to fill most of the space. Make your own by ripping 2-inch wide strips of ⅛-inch hardboard, and plywood that's ¼- and ½-inch thick. Crosscut the strips into 4-inch lengths with your miter saw. By combining these three thicknesses, you'll quickly fill the openings between the furring strips and ceiling. For fussy final adjustments or leveling, use tapered shims in pairs—install one from each side of the strip—so that you don't twist the wood.

## Drywall suspension system

A drywall ceiling suspension system is somewhat like the familiar dropped ceiling that accepts tiles, but the members are engineered for face-application of drywall—up to doubled ⅝-inch panels. You'll lose a few inches of ceiling height, but the metal system installs fast and produces flat framing for great results.

**3** Using a mason's line and a line level, transfer the bottom edge of the first furring strip to the opposite wall. Mark the second wall, and install the second furring strip level to the first one.

**4** String a nylon mason's line between the first top nails on the two strips. Hold a scrap piece of strip next to the string at the furring strip centerline marked on the ceiling. If the string is below the furring strip, ignore it for now. If the strip projects past the string, measure the amount, and write it on the ceiling. Record only the largest projection you find along the string. Move the string 12 inches, and repeat the process until you've checked the entire ceiling surface.

**5** When you've completed the previous step, the largest measurement indicates the lowest part of the ceiling. (If there are several spots with an identical measurement, you can start at any one of them.) Screw a furring strip flush against the ceiling at the low point, and shim its ends to level it. Now you have a level surface across the room. Remove the temporary strips at the ends of the room.

**6** Clip a line level onto a mason's line and run it from the bottom center of the first furring strip to the corners of the room, making pencil marks. Snap chalk lines on the walls connecting the corners.

**7** Install each furring strip by first shimming its ends flush with the chalk lines on the walls. Using a level or straightedge along the bottom of the strip, secure its midpoint. At the remaining attachment points, gently slide in the shims so that you don't bow the strip, then nail through the shims into the joists. Work carefully, checking that each new strip you install is straight and level with the previous one.

# CREATING SOUND CONTROL AND FIREWALLS

If you want to limit the amount of sound that escapes from a room, incorporate one or all of these five strategies into wall and ceiling construction.

■ Add sound-absorbing material into the stud or joist bays (Step 1).

■ Separate the two sides of the wall from each other. One way to do this is by screwing resilient steel channel to the wall or ceiling, then screwing the drywall to the channel. Other methods include staggering 2×4 studs on a 2×6 soleplate, or even framing two walls, then separating them with a 1-inch dead-air space. You'll gain additional isolation by gluing and screwing the second layer of drywall to the first, not to the framing (Step 2).

■ Increase the mass of the wall or ceiling by using thicker panels and/or installing multiple layers (Steps 3 and 4).

■ Install a sound-reduction board as the first layer and top it with drywall .

■ Seal sound pathways by caulking, gasketing electrical outlets, and weatherstripping doors (Step 5).

The irony of successfully decreasing sound transmission is that a room becomes more acoustically reflective. So you'll probably need to consider adding some sound-absorbing materials such as carpeting and drapes.

Consult with your local building officials before building a firewall to ensure that you utilize the correct materials and framing techniques.

**1** Install insulation in the stud cavities to dampen sound transmission. For this purpose, sound attenuation fire blankets (SAFB) are superior to fiberglass. The mineral fiber blankets stand up in stud bays without mechanical fastening. For ceiling applications, installing resilient channel first is a good plan.

**2** Screw resilient steel channels to the walls, spacing them 16 inches on center. You'll notice that the channel's design minimizes the amount of direct contact between the studs and the wallboard.

## INSTALL A SOUND-REDUCTION BOARD

A special type of wall panel is engineered to serve as the base layer instead of drywall in a two-layer sound-reduction installation. (One brand is Homasote 440 Sound Barrier Panel.) Following the manufacturer's instructions, install the panels vertically to wood or metal studs, using adhesive and screws. Top it with a layer of ⅝-inch drywall, secured with adhesive and No. 10×1½-inch type G screws driven into the base panel, not the studs.

**3** Install the first layer of drywall vertically, screwing it to the channels. To achieve the best sound control, make each layer of drywall as thick as possible; two applications of ⅝-inch panels produces excellent results. In high-end projects where even greater sound control is needed, you can use a third or even fourth layer.

**4** Apply adhesive to the back of the second layer and install it horizontally. Drive type G screws into the first drywall layer, avoiding both the studs and resilient channels. See *page 77* for advice on fastener spacing.

**5** Using a caulking gun and a special acoustical sealant, fill all cracks around the wall's perimeter, especially at the bottom of the wall. Also caulk any gaps between the drywall and electrical boxes and heat ducts.

### Batten down the outlets

After you've finished the wall, install closed-cell foam gaskets around electrical outlets and switches. The precut sheets are inexpensive and easy to install before you add the cover plates.

### X-rated drywall

Panels approved for fire-rated construction are called type X gypsum board. These sheets are usually ⅝-inch thick, although you may find ½-inch panels with the X designation. Check with your local building inspection officials before installation to ensure that you'll comply with code requirements.

### Seal holes in firewalls

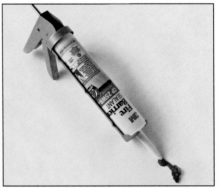

Even a small hole can compromise the effectiveness of a fire-rated wall. Seal small cracks and holes with a special fire-rated caulk. For larger cracks, or to seal around the penetration of pipes, choose fire-rated setting-type compound. This compound is sometimes tinted pink so that building inspectors can easily verify its use.

# CHECKING AND CORRECTING FRAMING

**L**umber can be notoriously mobile, especially during its first year inside a house. As the lumber dries, it shrinks across the grain. Other forces also hard at work include uneven grain, stresses that were built up in the living tree, and the loads imposed on the wood in its new role as dimensional lumber. As a result, studs and joists can bend, bow, twist, and cup—even after you've built a wall that was flat and plumb.

Ideally, you want to wait as long as possible after framing to begin drywall installation so that the wood has a chance to acclimate. But even if you have to rush, time spent checking and correcting framing problems will pay big dividends.

Although studs can often be straightened, the procedure is sometimes more trouble than it's worth. Ripping out the deformed stud and replacing it can be the most efficient solution. Another strategy—called sistering—involves installing a new stud next to the bad one.

## PRESTART CHECKLIST

☐ **TIME**
Checking an 8-foot length of wall, including a doorway, can be accomplished in as quickly as 5 minutes. The time required for repairs depends on their number and complexity.

☐ **TOOLS**
4-foot or longer level, straightedge, saw, plane, chisel, power screwdriver, nylon mason's line

☐ **SKILLS**
Using a level, sighting along a straightedge

☐ **PREP**
Construct framing

☐ **MATERIALS**
Shims, screws, nails, scrap lumber for bridging

**1** As a quick check, hold a straight piece of lumber horizontally and diagonally across the studs to check that their edges are in the same plane. A stud that's bowed outward makes the test board rock; an inward bow shows daylight between the stud's edge and the test board.

**2** If the stud bows outward, mark the edge of the stud with the amount to remove. Saw, plane, or chisel away the waste until the face of the stud is flat and in the same plane as its neighbors.

## Check openings carefully

Check each door opening to make sure that it's not cross-legged—an out-of-plane condition that make door installation very difficult. Diagonal strings from nails at the corners should just touch at the center. If the lines don't touch or press against each other, use a sledge hammer against the soleplate to nudge one or both walls into alignment. Getting the wall absolutely plumb is ideal, but if you have to compromise between flat and plumb, choose flat.

**3** Fill in the hollow of an inward-bowed stud with flat shims (see *page 56*). Check your progress with a straightedge held against the face of the stud. Thin shims let you achieve near-perfect alignments.

**4** If the stud bows to the side, force it into position with blocking that bridges at least the next two studs on each side. Staggering the blocking up and down makes it easy to drive nails or screws into the ends. Install the blocking into the neighboring studs first, reinforcing them against the strain of straightening.

**5** If you're working around a twisted wooden stud, coax it into alignment with a jumbo adjustable wrench or a special tool that's made for tweaking lumber into position. To ensure that the stud won't return to its old ways, drive some additional fasteners at the top and bottom and add blocking to the two neighboring studs.

**STANLEY** PRO TIP

### Thin shims

To remove the last $1/16$ inch of misalignment, buy a few squares of inexpensive self-adhesive floor tiles. Cut them into strips $1\frac{1}{2}$ inches wide and press them into position.

### Another straightening strategy

Note: Use this procedure only on studs in nonloadbearing walls. Start by slicing a saw kerf into the middle of the inward arc, cutting halfway to two-thirds through the stud. Drive a wedge into the kerf, pushing the stud straight. Reinforce the stud with 4-foot lengths of 1×4s (called scabs) nailed or screwed to both sides of the stud.

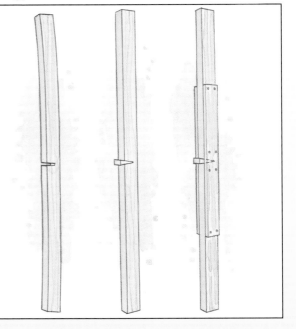

# MEASURING & CUTTING

In some ways, the process of cutting drywall defies logic. After all, you learned in the old game that scissors can cut paper but rock breaks scissors. So the idea that a blade can cut the rock of a drywall panel is mildly amazing.

The core of drywall is made from gypsum, a mineral that's mined from the earth. But gypsum is a relatively soft material, and it needs a paper backing and face to retain its shape. By slicing through the face paper and scoring partway into the gypsum core, you create a fault line. When you apply pressure along the back, the panel snaps. Cutting the back paper completes the cut.

## Making inside cuts

The score-and-snap technique works great for straight cuts, whether along the panel's length, width, or diagonally. But you need a different approach to make an inside cut. The manual method employs the jab saw. With a little practice, you'll become proficient.

A jab saw will cut an opening quickly, but not fast enough to suit a professional drywaller who is always in a race against the clock to make a profit. That's why many pros use a drywall router. After a practice session, you'll be able to cut openings for electrical boxes with accuracy and speed. You probably wouldn't win a race with a professional, but you'll get pro-quality results.

## Going around in circles

A jab saw will do an effective job of cutting circular openings for pipes and ceiling canisters. But if you're faced with the task of cutting a bunch of holes for ceiling canisters, choose from one of several tools that will speed your task. A manual circle cutter looks like an overgrown beam compass, and will quickly score the drywall. Another choice is a hole saw. The "Tools" chapter *(page 28)* provides more details.

## Accurate measuring, marking, and cutting leads to top-quality fit and finish.

### CHAPTER PREVIEW

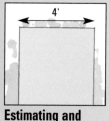
**Estimating and optimizing**
*page 64*

**Straight and angled cuts**
*page 66*

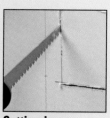
**Cutting in an electrical box (manual)**
*page 68*

**Cutting in an electrical box (router)**
*page 70*

**Cutting circles**
*page 72*

*Making a straight cut on a drywall panel is an extension—with one slight variation—of the old carpenter's adage: measure twice, cut once. Measure accurately, score the line of the cut on the front, and snap the panel back along the cut. Finish the job by cutting the back paper and snap the pieces forward. A drywall T-square makes the job easy.*

# ESTIMATING AND OPTIMIZING

**B**efore you order drywall for your project, take a little time to measure and sketch the ceiling and each wall. The few minutes it takes to develop the materials list and installation plan pays big dividends. First, you'll have a definite work strategy so you'll start hanging the drywall with confidence instead of scratching your head and making it up as you go along. Second, you'll minimize the length of seams, and that means less time and materials required for taping, mudding, and sanding. Third, you'll minimize—or even eliminate—time-consuming butt seams.

Whenever possible, cover small areas with a single sheet of drywall. The drawing of **Wall A** shows how you can seamlessly cover any surface that's equal to or smaller than a standard panel. Finishing the field of this panel will be straightforward because

you simply need to cover the heads of the fasteners.

### The horizontal guideline
Horizontal application of wall panels is a good idea for several reasons. By uniting more studs with a single sheet, you produce a stronger structure. The strength gains another boost because drywall is stronger along its grain than across it. (See *page 20* for more information on drywall grain direction.) You also don't have to be so concerned about perfect spacing of studs. (With vertical application it's an absolute necessity so that the panel's edge lands on the centerline of the studs.) And running an unbroken horizontal sheet above doors and windows minimizes the chances for stress cracks in coming years that can radiate from the corners of these openings.

But even if all those reasons weren't compelling enough, horizontal application reduces the length of seams you need to finish. Compare the drawings of **Wall B** and **Wall C,** and you'll see that vertical application generates 16 lineal feet of seams in the field of the panels; horizontal application cuts that down to 12 feet. While that may not seem like a dramatic reduction, you also need to consider the ease of application. To reach the full length of a vertical seam, you'll spend some of your time on a stepladder and some time down on your knees. With a horizontal seam, you get to keep both feet planted on the floor.

### Taming the tall wall
Soaring ceilings are a common feature in many older homes and are surging in popularity in new construction. Garages are

*Wall A*

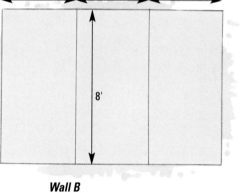

*Wall B*

*Vertical panel application is acceptable, but the horizontal seamline is 25 percent shorter and much easier to reach.*

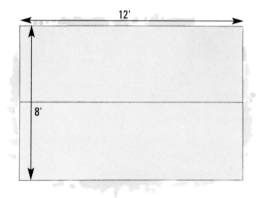

*Wall C*

*Wall D*

another area where you'll commonly find high walls.

Drywall panels that are 54 inches wide are a great choice for covering walls up to 9 feet high. When you compare the drawing of **Wall D** with **Wall E,** you'll discover a dramatic reduction in seam length: 18 feet for vertical application and only 10 feet for horizontal. One drawback: You probably won't find these wide panels in lengths over 12 feet.

### Butt seams—sometimes unavoidable

As the comparison of Walls D and E demonstrates, horizontal installation can sometimes make such a dramatic difference in finishing that getting longer sheets into your work site will pay dividends in reduced installation time. Even if you need to temporarily remove window sashes to stuff

panels through that opening, you'll probably still save time—plus have smoother walls.

But sometimes, small windows, narrow hallways, and other obstacles dictate the hanging of short panels. That makes butt joints unavoidable. Long walls are another reality that makes butt seams inevitable. You probably won't find a drywall panel longer than 16 feet, but that's just as well— you wouldn't be able to lift it anyway.

Despite the fact that butt seams are more difficult to finish than tapered edges, you'll still find that horizontal application makes sense. The drawing of **Wall F** shows 32 lineal feet of seams within the field. **Wall G** has 20 feet of edge seams and 8 feet of butt seams.

Note that the vertical butt seams in Wall G are staggered to make them less visible. To make the butt seams easier to hide,

consider using one of the back blocking techniques discussed on *page 65.*

### Optimizing the yield

When you compare the amount of trashed material to the amount that's installed, drywall is probably one of the most wasteful construction operations. But on a square-foot basis, it's probably the least expensive construction material in your house.

However, these two facts don't justify carelessness and wasteful working habits. When you're developing the installation plan, look for ways to juggle the commercially available lengths to minimize waste. If you were planning an installation like Wall D, your materials list would show two 16-foot panels and one 8-footer.

*Horizontal application can sometimes cut your finishing work nearly in half. Wall D has 18 lineal feet of seams in its field; Wall E has only 10 feet.*

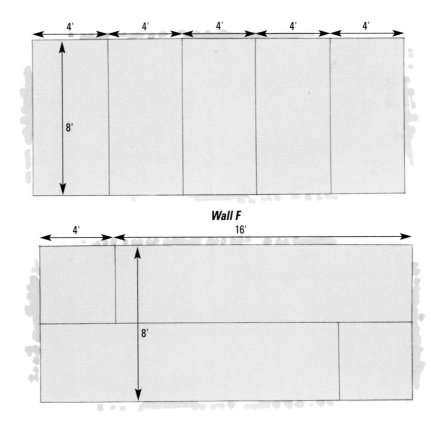

**Wall F**

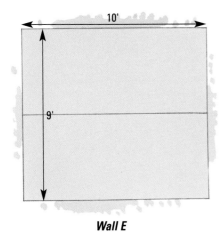

**Wall E**

**Wall G**

# STRAIGHT AND ANGLED CUTS

**C**utting drywall is surprisingly easy if you follow a few simple rules and develop consistent techniques.

First, make sure that you have a sharp blade in your utility knife. A sharp edge will slice the face paper cleanly and score the panel deeply enough for a clean break.

A dull blade will snag the paper, and as you push harder to try to make it cut you multiply the chances that the blade will slip and cut you. That's why it's said that a dull knife is more dangerous than a sharp one.

Second, make sure you keep your fingers well out of the knife's path—just in case it does slip. Position your free hand to the side of the cutline.

Third, make sure that straightedge is actually straight by sighting down its length. Check your drywall square by drawing a line across a drywall panel, using one factory edge as a reference. Switch the square to the opposite factory edge, and make sure that the blade aligns with the pencil line. If you can't adjust the square, buy a replacement.

## PRESTART CHECKLIST

☐ **TIME**
Allow approximately five minutes per marking, and cutting

☐ **TOOLS**
Utility knife and blades, tape measure, T square, pencil, jab saw (or drywall router)

☐ **SKILLS**
Measuring and marking, using a utility knife

☐ **MATERIALS**
Drywall panels

**1** Mark the piece about ¼ inch smaller than the space it needs to fit. Use a utility knife to cut through the outside face of the drywall and into the gypsum. Make a second pass to deepen the cut; you do not need to cut through the sheet.

**2** To complete the cut, bump the back of the sheet at the cutline with your knee as you hold the sheet. This will snap the gypsum so you can fold back the sheet. Slice the back paper along the fold line with a utility knife.

## Cut scrap strips to "fold" for easy disposal

Make a scoring cut though the face about 12 inches from one end, then a scoring cut through the back 12 inches from that. Alternate cuts on the front and back sides, and you can then fold up the strip like an accordion.

# Fitting angled pieces

**1** Rather than measuring the angle at which a piece must be cut, measure the length of the horizontal run and the vertical rise.

**2** Transfer the measurements to the drywall, then draw a cut line between the two marks. Cut and snap the piece along the line.

## WHAT IF...
### You have to cut drywall around a window or doorway?

Run the drywall right over door or window openings, and cut it after you've fastened the panel. Use a coarse-toothed saw to cut along the studs at both sides of a door opening, then score and snap the horizontal line.

With windows, you'll usually have to use a jabsaw to cut the entire perimeter. Simply cut along the studs until you reach the header, then make the horizontal cut. Of course, a drywall router speeds through the cuts needed at both doors and windows.

Although you might be tempted to create a seam above these openings, you'll get better results if you cover the opening with a single span of material. That's because an unbroken expanse of drywall can better resist the stresses that often occur at the corners of openings.

### Scribing drywall to fit

To cut a piece of drywall to fit against an irregular surface, hold the piece near the surface and trace the outline onto the sheet with a scribing tool.

# CUTTING IN AN ELECTRICAL BOX (MANUAL METHOD)

**S**ome people believe that accurate results require tedious measurement. But this procedure demonstrates how easy it is to get great results without squinting at a tape measure. In fact, once you've made the jigs for setting and marking the boxes, you can put your measuring equipment back into your toolbox.

The box-setting jig enables you to quickly position outlets at a uniform height and with a consistent projection from the framing. You then use the marking jig to transfer the position of each box to the floor, virtually guaranteeing that you'll never bury a box behind the drywall.

The marking jig then enables you to lay out the box's outline onto the face of the panel. Cutting the opening with your jab saw is a quick and confident process.

## PRESTART CHECKLIST

☐ **TIME**
Allow approximately five minutes per outlet box for setting, marking, and cutting

☐ **TOOLS**
Circular saw to make jigs, power drill/driver, jab saw, pencil, fine-line permanent marker

☐ **SKILLS**
Measuring and marking, using the jab saw

☐ **PREP**
Wiring must be installed and inspected, if required by local regulations

☐ **MATERIALS**
Plywood, 2×4, screws

**1** Make the jig for setting electrical boxes (see below), and use it when you nail the boxes to the studs to ensure uniformity. Rest the nail-on box atop the jig, and position its front edge flush with the plywood. After the wiring is completed (and inspected if necessary), install any other utilities behind the wall and add insulation if desired.

**2** Cut a square of ¾-inch plywood that matches the height of the top of the electrical boxes. Mark the bottom of the box on the plywood's edge. Use this jig to transfer the position of each electrical box and switch onto the floor. The circle with two lines drawn on the floor is the symbol for an outlet. A dollar sign is the symbol for a switch.

## Jig for setting electrical boxes

When you build the jig to the dimensions shown and use it on a wall with a 2×4 bottom plate, you'll position the bottom of electrical boxes 12 inches above the subfloor. Of course, you can alter the length of the 2×4 to shift the position of the box upward or downward. Plywood that's nominally ½ inch thick actually measures slightly less, so positioning the face of the box flush with the plywood means that the box will sit about 1/16 inch back from the face of ½-inch drywall, which is right where you want it. If the drywall is thicker or thinner, substitute plywood with a nominal thickness equal to the drywall.

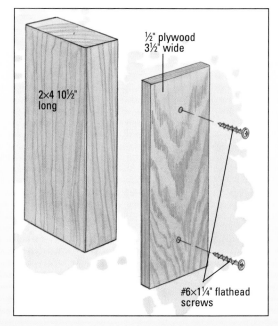

2×4 10½" long

½" plywood 3½" wide

#6×1¼" flathead screws

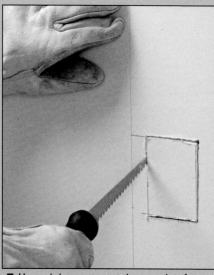

**3** Attach the drywall to the studs, but avoid any fasteners within 16 inches of each box. Using the plywood jig and the marks on the floor, draw the perimeter of each electrical box onto the drywall. Align the edge of the plywood with the right mark, and draw a pencil up the edge of the plywood and over its top end. Hold the pencil at the lower mark on the plywood, and slide it to the left until you reach the left mark on the floor. Draw up the edge of the plywood to complete the perimeter of the box.

**4** Use a jab saw to cut the opening for each box. Cutting about ⅛ inch outside of each line creates a enough clearance so that the drywall will fit easily. Pulling the edge of the drywall slightly away from the wall allows you to use a longer saw stroke. Keep the cut square to the surface of the drywall, and be careful that you don't snag any wires or nick the electrical insulation.

**5** The electrical outlet box should slide into the cutout, enabling you to complete the fastening of the drywall. If you need to make the opening bigger, you can easily see where to cut. If you overcut the opening, see *page 135* for a repair procedure. Drive nails or screws to complete the fastening of the drywall.

## WHAT IF...
### You want to set a box between studs?

Sometimes the aesthetics of a room—or simple convenience—dictates that an outlet box must be at a precise location that's not immediately next to a stud. Although you can solve this problem by adding framing members, an "old work" electrical box is an efficient answer.

First, run the wiring to the stud bay, and coil an extra length of wire to make it easy to grab later. For safety, cap each conductor of the wire with a separate wire nut or tape. After you attach the drywall, cut a hole for the box. You can trace the outline of the box onto the wall or get a free paper template from the store where you buy the electrical box.

Pull the wires through the hole, thread them into the box, and set the box into its opening. Rotating the mounting screws of the box turns "ears" that press against the back surface of the drywall to securely hold the box.

# CUT IN AN ELECTRICAL BOX (ROUTER METHOD)

**P**eople who hang drywall for a living will tell you that speed is the all-important difference between making a living and going hungry. So the fact that most pro drywallers cut electrical box openings with a router speaks volumes.

Of course, you won't achieve high-speed results with the first opening you cut, but you'll be pleasantly surprised how quickly you develop a feel for the process.

Get some practice with the new tool before you commit to a full sheet of drywall. Temporarily screw a piece of scrap drywall over an electrical box, then cut the opening. Shift the drywall to a new position, and keep trying until you become confident of your new skills.

To control the dust—an important consideration in remodeling projects—purchase a dust hood accessory for your router. Hook it up to your shop vac, and you'll dramatically reduce jobsite mess. The fine dust can quickly choke your vac, so clean the filter often.

**1** Chuck a piloted drywall bit into the router, and set the tool on a piece of drywall so that the bit overhangs the edge. Loosen the depth-of-cut adjustment knob, and set the bit so that it will cut about ⅛ inch deeper than the drywall's thickness. Securely lock this setting.

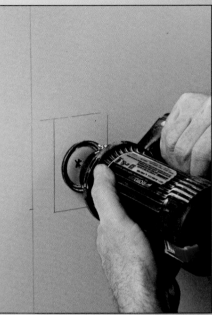

**2** Shove the wiring as far back as possible in the electrical box. Hang the sheet of drywall into position, but keep all fasteners about 16 inches away from the box so that the wallboard won't crack when you make the cut. Mark the approximate centerpoint of the box and plunge the running bit at this mark.

## PRESTART CHECKLIST

☐ **TIME**
With even a little experience, you'll cut an electrical box opening in less than one minute.

☐ **TOOLS**
Drywall router with piloted bit

☐ **SKILLS**
Operating a router

☐ **PREP**
Mark the location of electrical boxes on the floor; shove wiring to the back of the box

☐ **MATERIALS**
The usual set of tools needed for hanging drywall

## Protect the wiring

Switch boxes are often at the seam line of drywall that's applied horizontally. While that makes the box opening easy to cut, it also means that the wires can get encased in joint compound when you tape and mud the joint.

To avoid a messy cleanup chore, shove all the wires as far back into the box as possible. Then cut a piece of corrugated cardboard to fit snugly into the box, and jam it into place. Leave the cardboard in position through all the finishing and painting steps. When you pop out the protective layer to install the switches, the wires will be clean.

**3** Move the router to your right until you feel the bit contact the edge of the box. Tip the router slightly backward as you continue to move the tool about ¼ inch to the right. This move jumps the bit over the edge of the electrical box. Return the router to its perpendicular position, and slide it slightly left until you feel the bit touch the outside of the box.

**4** Move the tool counterclockwise around the perimeter of the electrical box, keeping the bit in constant light contact with the box. When you complete the cut, withdraw the bit and shut off the tool. Set it down where the bit can't strike anything while it coasts to a stop.

**5** The electrical box should slide into the cutout, enabling you to complete the fastening of the drywall. If you need to make the opening bigger, you can easily see where to cut. You can use the drywall router or jabsaw to make the adjustment. If you overcut the opening, see *page 135* for a repair procedure.

### How do I control the dust?

Drywall routers have high-speed motors that excel at two things: fast cutting and kicking up clouds of dust. Fortunately some drywall routers offer a dust hood as an optional accessory. When you connect the chute of the hood to a 1¼-inch shop vac hose, you have an effective dust-collection system.

Several cautions are in order. First, be sure to wear hearing protection when you operate this system. The combination of the shop vac and router produces a noise level that's literally deafening. Second, clean the shop vac filter regularly to maintain maximum efficiency.

### Another way to mark a box

Here's another way to mark the location of an electrical box. On the plus side, it has extreme accuracy. On the negative side, it requires you to remove the drywall to cut the opening.

Smear a thin coating of powdered chalk onto the face of the outlet box. (This photo shows a finger applying chalk to the face of the electrical box. The other hand holds the chalk line reel with its fill slot open.) Position the drywall in its exact installed position, then firmly tap the drywall with your fist to transfer the chalk to the back of the panel. Remove the drywall panel, and place it face down on sawhorses.

You may need to trace the perimeter of the chalk mark with a pencil to make it easier to see. Cut the opening with a jab saw, cutting one blade width to the outside of the line. Replace the panel on the wall, and fasten it. Some people may suggest using lipstick as a transfer medium, but most formulations contain oils that could cause adhesion problems with wall paint.

# CUTTING CIRCLES

**C**utting circular openings for ceiling canisters or other electrical boxes can sometimes be quite easy. If the canister is within a couple of feet of the edge of the drywall, you can hoist the drywall into position and reach between the joists to trace the can's perimeter onto the back of the drywall panel. Of course, a drywall lift is a valuable helper in this process.

But if you can't reach the canister, you can utilize the procedure outlined here to produce professional results.

Making the jig takes a few minutes' time, and it's a tool that will last through many remodeling projects. You probably have enough material in your scrap bin to make it, so its cost is virtually nothing.

## PRESTART CHECKLIST

☐ **TIME**
Working with a helper, about 5 minutes per ceiling canister

☐ **TOOLS**
Tape measure, compass, jigsaw, plumb bob with nylon line, permanent marker, drywall lift (optional but recommended)

☐ **SKILLS**
Accurate measuring, using a plumb bob

☐ **PREP**
Install ceiling canisters and have wiring inspected, if necessary

☐ **MATERIALS**
Scrap plywood and 1×2s, screw eye, ceiling canister with supplied hole template

**1** Measure the inside diameter of your ceiling canister and use a compass to draw a circle of that size onto a piece of ¼-inch plywood. Carefully cut the circle with your jigsaw, and drill a ⅛-inch hole at the center. Also drill a hole in the perimeter of the circle. Nail the disc to a pair of 1×2 strips so the assembly won't fall into the canister. Attach one end of a nylon mason's line to a plumb bob (or use a chalk line and case) and thread the other end into the center hole and out through the perimeter hole. By pulling on the free end of the line, you can adjust the line's length while the plumb bob stays centered.

**2** Recruit a helper for the next steps. One person working at the canister adjusts the length of the string so that the plumb bob is as close to the floor as possible without touching it. The other person steadies the plumb bob until it settles. Make a dot on the floor with a permanent marker at the tip of the plumb bob, then draw a circle around the mark so that you don't misplace it.

## Using a circle cutter

You can utilize a beam-type circle cutter in two different ways. In the first method, you're essentially using it as a compass, and in the second procedure you score both sides. Both procedures start the same way. Slide the beam to the diameter you want, then turn the knob above the pivot to lock the setting. Put the pivot point into the drywall, and press the cutter firmly to score the face paper. If you're using the cutter as a compass, complete the cut with a jab saw.

To complete the hole with the cutter, press the pivot point all the way through the drywall to mark the center on the back of the panel. You may need to adjust the pivot's projection with a setscrew in the shaft. Repeat the scoring cut on the back of the drywall. A few sharp hammer blows from the front of the panel will pop out the circle.

## Cutting small circles

A jab saw will quickly cut small circular openings, but a hole saw in a drill gives results that are neater and faster. Hardware stores and home centers stock hole saws in a wide range of sizes, so you're almost certain to find one that matches your needs.

**3** Put the drywall panel for the ceiling onto a lift and carefully position it against the joists. Don't exert too much pressure, or you could crack the panel. Thread the plumb bob's line through a small screw eye, and use its tip to transfer the mark on the floor onto the drywall panel. Again, you'll benefit by having a helper working at floor level.

**4** Lower the ceiling panel several inches to make it easier to cut. Get the hole template that's usually furnished with the ceiling canister. Center the template, and draw its perimeter with a pencil. If you don't have a template, measure the canister, then mark the circle with a compass. Using your jab saw, cut to the outside of the line so the fit isn't too snug.

**5** Raise the panel against the ceiling joists, carefully steering it into position. Drive nails or screws to hold the drywall panel in place. Miscuts with ceiling canisters are usually not a serious problem because the trim ring will conceal a flawed fit. But if you have a serious miscut, refer to the repair procedure for miscut outlets on *page 135.*

## A specialized saw speeds circle cutting

Buy an adjustable hole saw, and you'll breeze through the cutting steps. The saw shown here adjusts from 2½-inch to 7-inch diameter in ½-inch increments. You can also purchase fixed-diameter hole saws, and some of these have replaceable blades for increased longevity. Another plus of a fixed-diameter blade is that you don't have to worry about the setting working its way loose.

You'll probably find a good selection of hole cutters stocked in the electrical tool section of your home center.

## Remodeling canister installs fast

Ceiling canisters designed for new construction mount to the ceiling joists and require the careful marking procedures described above. But if you choose a remodeling-type canister, you'll simplify matters because you cut the opening after installing the panels to the ceiling. You'll still

need to mark canister locations on the floor to ensure that you position them accurately, but you'll dramatically lower the overall level of difficulty. Run the wiring to the desired location, and coil a few feet of wire to ensure that you'll have enough to make the connections. Support the coil well above the lower edge of the joist so that the wire won't get pinched between the drywall and joist. After you install the panel to the ceiling, mark and cut the opening for the canister. Make the wiring connections at the fixture's junction box and slip the canister into its opening. Pressing clips inside the cylinder secures the fixture to the ceiling panel. If the ceiling contains insulation, be sure you select a fixture with an IC (insulation contact) designation. Installing a non-IC fixture could build up dangerous levels of heat.

# BASIC DRYWALL HANGING

**H**anging drywall is a process that moves a construction or remodeling project into an entirely new phase. After the preparatory stages of planning, framing, and installation of utilities, drywall quickly initiates the transformation from job site to living space. You may have spent weeks or even months imagining a ceiling and walls. All right! Reality is just around the corner.

### Enlist some help

If you're installing panels on a ceiling, seriously consider renting a drywall lift or at least building some deadman supports. Manually hoisting panels can be an exhausting chore that dampens your enthusiasm right from the get-go. Recruit at least one helper, and thoroughly discuss the lifting, holding, and fastening processes before you touch your first sheet of drywall. Having different strategies while holding drywall over your head isn't a good idea.

### Get the right fasteners

Choosing the right fasteners and adhesive for your project is crucial for a quality long-lasting project. Fortunately it's an easy process—simply refer to the chart and tips on pages 23 and 77 to guide your selection. If you choose nails, make sure that you get the ringshank variety for maximum holding power. If you opt for screws, make certain that you select the correct thread pattern: drive coarse type W threads into wood framing, fine type S threads into steel studs and resilient channels, and extra-coarse type G threads for gypsum-to-gypsum wallboard laminations.

### Follow some guidelines

Experienced drywallers can drive fasteners along the length of a stud or joist and rarely miss. But most mere mortals need the benefit of guidelines lightly penciled or a drywall square. You can also mark with a chalk line if you do a preliminary snap on the floor to remove most of the chalk. After that, you can snap several lines that are lightly visible but still easy to wipe away with a rag.

## Attaching drywall transforms all the planning and prep into a real room.

### CHAPTER PREVIEW

**Adhesives, screws, and nails**
*page 76*

**Covering a ceiling**
*page 78*

**Covering walls**
*page 82*

**Butt joints**
*page 84*

*Carefully plan your drywall installation sequence, and you'll install the panels quickly and efficiently. A few special tools and some new products make this job progress more quickly and with less effort than in the past.*

**Gypsum and cementious backerboards**
*page 86*

# ADHESIVES, SCREWS, AND NAILS

**A**dhesives, screws, or nails: Which one do you choose? If you're working with wood studs, you may need all three. With steel studs, you may combine adhesive with screws.

Adhesive has several excellent properties that justify its modest cost. When you use panel adhesive, you'll reduce the number of fasteners required, as shown in the chart on *page 77.* That means you'll have fewer fastener heads to mud and sand, reducing materials and work while producing a smoother surface. In addition, adhesive keeps the panel solidly bonded to the framing, so you won't need to contend with drywall that rattles against the studs.

But there are some cases where you can't use adhesive. One example is when you cover exterior walls with plastic sheeting for a vapor barrier.

Even if you plan to use screws for your project, you should have a few nails on hand. They work great for quickly tacking a panel to the wall or ceiling so you can release your grip.

For professional drywallers, screws are the fastener of choice because they're fast and resist popping. You can equip your driver/drill with an inexpensive dimpler that automatically countersinks the head without breaking the surface of the paper. For even finer control of depth, buy or rent a drywall screwgun. (You'll also find that it's handy for assembling wood projects.) For the ultimate in speed and one-handed operation, purchase a driver that accepts screws collated on plastic strips. It makes driving screws incredibly fast and easy. In the "Tools" chapter (see *page 28*), you'll also see a collated-strip accessory that adapts to your screwgun.

You can get excellent results on a nail-only project if you follow some easy guidelines: Choose ringshank nails in the length recommended by the chart, use a drywall hammer that produces a shallow crater, resist the urge to drive the nails too deeply, and remove all nails that miss the framing.

**1** After you cut the nozzle, apply drywall adhesive to the work area. Consult the manufacturer's instructions, but the usual application rate is ⅜-inch bead applied along the middle of each stud or joist. Where two sheets land on the same framing member, apply a double bead, with each one about ⅜ inch from the edge of the wood. On walls, don't apply adhesive to the top or bottom horizontal plates. Apply only to the studs, starting 6 inches from the ceiling and ending 6 inches from the floor.

**2** Position the panel and press it firmly in place. With some adhesives, you can drive nails or screws immediately. Other adhesives suggest that you pull the drywall back for a few minutes, then press it back into place for improved joint strength. Consult the directions on the tube. Don't get too far ahead of yourself when applying adhesive. A bead that's over 15 minutes old has lost enough solvent to weaken the bond.

## CUT THE NOZZLE

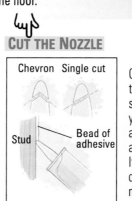

Chevron   Single cut

Stud    Bead of adhesive

Cut the nozzle to a chevron shape and you'll produce a neat bead along studs. If you have difficulty making the second cut in a downward motion, use your utility knife in a whittling stroke toward the tip of the spout. Keep one edge of the chevron against the stud as shown in the drawing, and you'll lay down a consistent bead.

For ceiling application, use a single cut to reduce the risk that the adhesive will fall before you place the panel. With the single cut, you'll apply adhesive as more of a smear than a bead.

## Reaching the right depth

Driving fasteners too deeply is a mistake that beginners often make. Overdriven fasteners weaken the connection. Whether you use

nails or screws, the goal is to set the head below the face of the panel without breaking the face paper. A special drywall hammer with a domed face creates a neat dimple instead of tearing paper as an ordinary hammer can.

Set the fastener just below the surface of the panel. One drywall manufacturer suggests that the head should be set a maximum of 1/32 inch. To check your work, lightly push a drywall knife over a fastener. If the blade doesn't snag on the head, you've driven deeply enough.

**3** Fasten the drywall with nails or screws according to the chart (right). Be sure that you push the panel firmly against the framing member when driving the fastener—don't rely on the fastener to pull the drywall against the wood. Also make certain that you don't break the panel's paper by driving the fasteners too deeply.

**4** Tap the edge of your fist along each framing member to ensure that the adhesive makes firm contact with the back of the drywall. If the panel flexes outward after you tap it down, add another fastener at that point. Allow the adhesive to cure for 48 hours before taping the joints.

## FASTENER SPACING CHART

| Framing | Application | Fastener type | Location | Spacing (in.) |
|---|---|---|---|---|
| **Wood** (framing at 16 inch centers | Single layer, fastener only | Nails | Ceiling<br>walls | 7 in.<br>8 in. |
| | | Screws | Ceiling<br>Walls | 12 in.<br>16 in. (see note 1) |
| | | Screws into resilient channels | Ceiling or walls | 12 in. |
| | Single layer, adhesive and fasteners | Nails or screws | Ceiling (perpendicular to joists) | 16 in. o.c.*at ends, one fastener per joist at mid-width |
| | | | Ceiling (parallel to joists) | 16 in. o.c. *at ends, 24 in. o.c. along joists |
| | | | Walls (perpendicular to studs) | 16 in. o.c.* at ends, one fastener per stud at mid-width |
| | Base layer of double layer, both applied with fasteners only | Nails or screws | Ceiling or walls | 24 in. |
| | Face layer of double layer, both applied with fasteners only | Nails | Ceiling<br>Walls | 7 in.<br>8 in. |
| | | Screws | Ceiling<br>Walls | 12 in.<br>16 in. |
| | Base layer of double layer, face layer applied with adhesive | Nails | Ceiling<br>Walls | 7 in.<br>8 in. |
| | | Screws | Ceiling<br>Walls | 12 in.<br>16 in. |
| | Face layer of double layer, face layer applied with adhesive | Nails or screws | Ceiling<br>Walls | 16 in. o.c.* at ends, one fastener per stud at mid-width top and bottom (see note 2) |
| **Steel** (framing at 24 inch centers) | Single layer | Screws | Ceiling<br>Walls | 12 in.<br>16 in. (see note 1) |
| | Base layer of double layer, both applied with fasteners only | Screws | Ceiling<br>Walls | 16 in.<br>24 in. |
| | Face layer of double layer, both applied with fasteners only | Screws | Ceiling<br>Walls | 12 in.<br>16 in. |
| | Base layer of double layer, face layer applied with adhesive | Screws | Ceiling<br>walls | 12 in.<br>16 in. |
| | Face layer of double layer, face layer applied with adhesive | Screws | Ceiling<br><br><br>Walls | 16 in. o.c.* at ends, one fastener per joist at mid-width top and bottom<br>Top and bottom (see note 2) |

*o.c. = on center (from the center of one fastener to the center of another)
Note 1: For water-resistant panels, space fasteners 12 in. o.c.
Note 2: For pre-bowed panels, fasten only the top and bottom edges of panel, using only as many fasteners as required to flatten panels. For flat panels, use temporary nails or type G screws as required to hold sheet until adhesive cures.

# COVERING A CEILING

**U**nlike your work career, you start at the top when you're installing drywall panels. You always install the ceiling before the walls.

Professional drywall crews make the process look easy. Two or more workers grab a panel that's leaning against the wall, and in a single motion they flip it horizontal, step onto short platforms, and press the panel against the joists. A split second later, they're supporting the panel with their heads, freeing their hands to drive screws. It's a smoothly choreographed routine they've performed thousands of times.

But you can get great results on your own ceiling even if you and your helper are both novices. To relieve the strain of holding the heavy panels overhead, make some deadman braces like those shown below. Or rent a drywall lift. Whichever route you select, helpers take a lot of the strain out of the project.

## PRESTART CHECKLIST

☐ **TIME**
Two to three hours for a flat ceiling in a 10×12-foot room

☐ **TOOLS**
Deadman braces or drywall lift, hammer or screwgun, tape measure, drywall T-square, chalk line, utility knife

☐ **SKILLS**
Measuring and cutting drywall, driving fasteners

☐ **PREP**

☐ **MATERIALS**
Drywall panels, adhesive, nails or screws

**1** For maximum strength and sag resistance, run ceiling panels perpendicular to the joists whenever possible. Cut the first panel to length, and mark light pencil lines across the panel to indicate the centerline of each joist. Partially start a few drywall nails near the center of the panel so you'll be able to attach it quickly after hoisting it into position. For photographic clarity, we darkened the pencil lines so that you can see them clearly. But you'll make the lines on your panels very lightly.

**2** If you apply adhesive to the joists, stop about 6 inches from the wall and 6 inches from the edge of the drywall. The first panel goes into a corner. Deadman braces help hold the ceiling panel until you can drive the fasteners.

### DEADMAN BRACES

Deadman braces, which provide strong support while you secure drywall to the ceiling, are easy to make. Although you might be able to get by with only one, you'll find that a pair is much more useful. If you're working with drywall over 10 feet long, you may want three deadmen.

Construction is dead easy—you don't even have to attach the 2×4 post and crossarm together. Simply butt these two pieces, and nail or screw the plywood gussets in place. To eliminate calculating the length of the post before assembly, cut it to length afterward. You can simply invert the brace, place the post next to a joist, and mark the cutline 1 inch above the bottom of the joist.

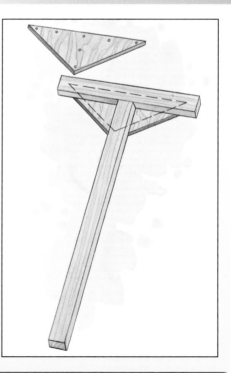

**3** Recruit a helper or two to assist you in lifting and positioning the drywall. Rest a deadman against a wall at the corner where you'll start installation. The top of the crossarm should be about 2 inches below the bottom of the joists. Lift one end of the panel onto the top of the crossarm, and kick the bottom of the brace toward the wall to hold the panel firmly. But don't overdo the pressure or you'll risk cracking the panel. Walk toward your helper as you both raise the opposite end of the panel.

**4** Support the panel by yourself for a moment while your helper grabs the other deadman brace. Positioning the brace about 2 feet from the end of the panel, the helper then lifts the panel against the joist. The helper lightly kicks the bottom of the post, moving it toward vertical to support the panel against the joists.

## Drywall lift safety

A drywall lift takes a lot of the heavy lifting out of installing a ceiling. But like nearly any tool, it can hurt you if you don't know how to use it properly.

If you rent a drywall lift, have the store personnel explain its assembly and operation. Learn how to tip the platform to horizontal and how to lock it in that position. Also be sure that you know how to extend the support arms that stabilize long sheets of material.

But be particularly certain that you understand how to safely raise and lower the column. Be sure that you always have a firm grip on the handle that sticks out from the elevating wheel. If you unlock the elevating mechanism without having total control of the wheel, the lift and its contents can fall suddenly, and the wheel will spin rapidly. You can suffer serious injuries—particularly to your head and hands.

## Use clips with trusses

If your ceiling consists of a truss system, place inexpensive drywall clips on the panel before you lift it in place. Screw or nail the clips to the wall studs. The clips are made for both ½- and ⅝-inch thick drywall and virtually eliminate the cracking that can occur at the wall/ceiling joint because of seasonal truss uplift. Put the first screw in the truss joist 12 inches from the wall.

If you want to skip the clips, create a floating joint by screwing into the truss joist no closer than 18 inches to the wall. In this case, the wall panels alone support the joint at the ceiling.

You can also use drywall clips to eliminate the expense of additional framing lumber at T-joints in non-structural interior walls, as shown on *page 52.*

# Covering a ceiling *(continued)*

**5** Check the panel to see if you need to fine-tune the fit. The long tapered edge should lightly touch the wall, and the end in the corner should be about ¼ inch from the wall. You need the clearance at the end of the panel because you'll start fastening at its middle. As you work toward the wall, you'll remove the sag in the sheet, and the gap will close. If you started with a tight fit at the corner, you would stress and bow the panel. To move the panel, both you and your helper get up on ladders. Support the panel with your head and one hand while your other hand releases the deadman. Move the panel, then replace the braces. Move the first brace several feet from the end wall to better support the panel.

**6** Move your ladder to the middle of the panel, and drive the nails you started earlier to secure the panel. Be sure you push the panel tightly against the joist before you drive the fastener. Referring to the fastener spacing chart on *page 77,* nail or screw the panel to the joists. Work from the center toward one end, then the other. You don't need to nail all the way to the edges of the panel near the wall because installing panels on the wall helps support the ceiling. In fact, if the framing lumber is not completely dry, consider the "floating" technique described below left.

## Creating a straight ceiling joint

Peaked ceilings and the joint between a sloped ceiling and wall are serious problem areas. The framing lumber may have bows or twists, so it's virtually impossible to achieve a perfectly straight joint line. In addition, the lumber will shrink and move as it dries, creating even further problems.

If you're faced with these problems, try attaching a heavy-gauge metal strip to the joists. One product, X-Crack (see "Resources" *page 139*), creates a joint line that stays straight despite the fact that the framing isn't straight now or even if it moves later.

The screwing pattern shown in the drawing creates a floating joint that permits the framing and drywall to move independently to avoid problems. Note that the last screw in the drywall field attaches it to a joist 8 to 12 inches from the metal. The next screw attaches the drywall to the metal but does not go into the joist.

You can bend the metal by hand to match the angle required in a number of applications: vaulted ceiling to wall, tepee ceilings, and many other off-angle applications.

Imagine that someone lifted the roof sheathing from your house to expose this view of a peaked ceiling. The metal strip creates a straight joint, and driving the screws as shown in the drawing creates a floating joint that's crack resistant.

Screws into metal strip

**7** Follow the same lift-and-brace techniques to install the next panel in the row. But this time, begin the fastening at the butt seam and work toward the free end of the panel. Don't worry about getting an absolutely tight fit between the ends of the panels. If the gap is ⅛ inch or less, you'll simply apply tape and joint compound over it. You'll need to fill gaps of ¼ inch or more before taping, following the procedure on *page 92*.

**8** Staggering the butt joints in the ceiling makes the ceiling stronger. Offset the butt joints by 2 feet or more whenever possible. You can often use the offcut from the first row of ceiling panels to start the second row. Another method is to start the second row at the opposite end of the room. For methods that help conceal butt joints in ceilings and walls, see *page 96*.

## Rock-clips

The Rock-clip screws to the tapered edge of drywall to help support the panel in the next row. The curved shape of the clip makes it easy to insert and position the sheet. As you fasten each panel, you simply unscrew the clips and re-use them for the next sheet. The Rock-clip is manufactured by Strait-Flex (see "Resources" on *page 139*).

WHAT IF...
## You have a cracked or wavy ceiling?

Cracked plaster ceilings are very common, and some homeowners don't consider them a defect. Instead, they see the cracks as character lines that are part of the charm of owning an older home. Other people, however, find the cracks bothersome and unsightly. If you're part of the second group and your ceiling is reasonably flat, consider covering it with a layer of drywall as shown at right.

Another approach involves removing the old ceiling and attaching fresh drywall directly to the joists. Removing a plaster ceiling is not particularly difficult, but it is messy and labor intensive. However, it may be a good choice if you want to add insulation between the joists.

If the ceiling sags or is wavy, you may have structural issues such as a broken joist. In that case, you'll have to get into the attic for an inspection or tear away part of the ceiling to diagnose the problem. If you have any doubts about the soundness of the framing, contact a structural engineer.

Resilient steel channels or furring strips allow you to create a flat plane that ensures your new ceiling will be free of waves and dips. You can also utilize a steel framework to make a flat attachment grid for new drywall.

Adding a layer of ⅜-inch drywall is an excellent way to restore a cracked or discolored plaster ceiling. Poke nails through the old ceiling until you locate all the joists (work carefully, there may be pipes or wires present), then snap lines along their length. Apply construction adhesive to the back of the sheet. Use about half a tube of adhesive per sheet, applying it in S-shape beads about 1 foot apart. Fasten with 2½-inch drywall screws into the joists.

# COVERING WALLS

Installing wall panels horizontally unites more studs, producing a stronger wall. This installation plan also allows the use of long panels, which can significantly reduce the lineal footage of seams, saving both materials and time. For more on the advantages of horizontal installation, see *page 64*.

If a panel fits tightly, don't crush it into a corner or try to hammer it into place. That can blow out the drywall or rip the face paper, requiring a time-consuming repair. Gaps of ⅛ inch between panels are perfectly acceptable. But if the gap reaches ¼ inch in width, you'll have to fill it with setting-type compound before taping (see *page 92*).

At first, the process of cutting for electrical boxes may intimidate you, but you'll get great results if you take a methodical approach and don't rush (see *page 68*).

The step-by-step installation is shown here on a wood stud wall. If your wall is made from metal studs, follow the special fastening process detailed on *page 84*.

## PRESTART CHECKLIST

☐ **TIME**
15 to 30 minutes per panel; variable by size and complexity of cuts

☐ **TOOLS**
Hammer or screwgun, tape measure, drywall T-square, chalk line, utility knife

☐ **SKILLS**
Measuring and cutting drywall, driving fasteners

☐ **PREP**
Framing completed, all utilities installed and inspected if necessary; insulation installed if needed

☐ **MATERIALS**
Drywall panels, adhesive, nails or screws

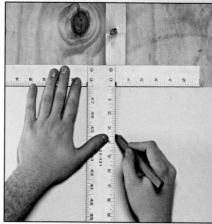

**1** Measure and cut the top board to length. If the panel doesn't run the entire length of the room, cut it at the midpoint of a stud to create a butt joint. If you use back blocking (see *page 85*), cut the panel so it ends at the midpoint of a stud bay. Lean the panel against the wall and transfer the centerline of each stud to the face of the drywall with a pencil mark. Using your drywall square, make a light pencil line on the panel to show you where to drive the screws or nails. We've exaggerated the darkness of the lines for photographic clarity, but you'll make your marks much fainter.

**2** Start a couple of drywall fasteners into the panel, and recruit an assistant to help you lift it into position. It's more important to have a snug fit at the top of the wall/ceiling joint than in the corner. In fact, leaving a ¼-inch gap from the end of the panel to the corner framing is fine for the first sheet—it eliminates stresses that could crack the corner. You don't have to ram the panel into place—light contact is sufficient. Partially drive several nails so that you can release the panel.

## WHAT IF...
### You're using adhesive?

Applying adhesive is an optional step that reduces the number of fasteners, and that means less work in filling and sanding holes. Snap a chalk line across the studs that indicates the width of the top panel. Start the adhesive 6 inches from the ceiling and stop it about 2 inches from the chalk line.

## Prebow panels for a tight fit

Prebowing wall panels is an effective way to ensure that the drywall snugs up against each stud. The procedure is extremely easy: Simply stack the drywall sheets face up, supporting each end on a pair of 2×4s. Gravity and time do the rest of the work for you. Let the sheets set at least overnight, although you may want to give them a full day to take on the curve.

When you install a prebowed panel, it flattens neatly against the framing, ensuring a snug fit. The technique is especially helpful if you use adhesive because the drywall rolls onto each stud, spreading the adhesive for full coverage.

**3** Start driving the fasteners into a stud at the approximate center of the panel's length. Refer to the chart on *page 77* for the correct fastener spacing. Drive fasteners down the center stud, working from top to bottom. Move to the next stud and work your way to the corner. Repeat the process along each stud from the center toward the free end.

**4** If you need to create a butt joint, lift the panel into place, and position it so it lightly touches the end of the first panel. Trying to shove the panels too tightly together will merely stress both of them, inviting a joint that bulges. Begin nailing along the stud at the butt joint, and work toward the free end. Be sure you drive the nails or screws squarely.

**5** Installing the bottom horizontal panel follows many of the same steps you used for the top. Be sure that butt joints in the top and bottom panels are offset by at least one stud. If you have to cut down the width of the lower panel, position the cut edge at the bottom. Take several measurements from the bottom of the upper board to the floor to ensure that you'll have at least ½ inch of clearance between the lower panel and the subfloor. A foot-operated panel lifter elevates the panel so tapered edges meet.

---

### Fitting into imperfect corners

Scribe drywall to fit a corner that's not perfectly vertical. Hold the piece near the corner and trace the contour onto the sheet with a compass/scribe. Cut with a drywall saw. If needed, trim the edge with a Surform® plane.

### REFRESHER COURSE
### Drive nails or screws squarely

When driving screws into a narrow surface (at a butt joint, for example), it's tempting to drive them at an angle. But doing so will weaken the joint by breaking the face paper. Driving nails or screws too close to the edge of a panel invites a blowout—the gypsum core cracks, expanding it past the end of the panel. Keep fasteners at least ⅜ inch from the drywall's edge to help avoid this problem.

### WHAT IF...
### You're hanging drywall vertically?

If you need to hang drywall sheets vertically, carefully check the framing before you begin to ensure that every panel edge will land squarely along the centerline of a stud. Also be certain that you get the edges of the first panel absolutely vertical. That way you'll ensure that subsequent panels will install squarely.

# BUTT JOINTS

**O**rdinary butt joints are difficult to conceal. That's because the ends of drywall panels—unlike the edges—are not tapered. As a result, you have a seam that's at the finished level of the wall and still requires tape and compound to make it disappear. The risk, of course, is that you'll end up with a mounded joint.

You avoid that by applying a minimal thickness directly over the seam and then working away from the joint with a gradual buildup of compound that makes it hard to see. For more details, see *page 92*.

But prevention is much easier than cure. There are inexpensive back blocking products you can buy—or even make—that convert a butt joint into a recessed seam, making it much easier to conceal with tape and compound. If you're a beginner, back blocking is the preferred route because it gives you the best chance of producing a flat wall.

Back blocking isn't just for walls. The technique works well for ceiling panels too. Always use screws to fasten the panels to the back blocker.

**1** When you use a back blocker, stop the drywall approximately in the center of a stud bay and slide the product behind the panel. If the stud bay is 16 inches or wider, you'll be able to position the metal legs perpendicular to the center wood strip. If the stud bay is narrower, rotate the metal legs as far as needed to fit.

**2** Center the back blocker along the end of the drywall, and drive screws 6 inches apart to secure it. Make certain that your fasteners miss the metal legs. With a pencil, draw the location of the legs onto the face of the panel.

## PRESTART CHECKLIST

☐ **TIME**
Using a back blocker will probably add five or fewer minutes to each butt joint

☐ **TOOLS**
Power drill/driver or drywall screwgun

☐ **SKILLS**
Driving screws

☐ **PREP**
Have tools and materials at job site

☐ **MATERIALS**
Drywall panels, purchased or homebuilt back blocker

**REFRESHER COURSE**
### Hanging drywall on metal studs

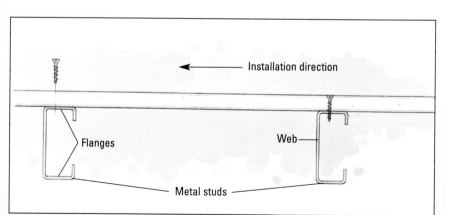

Installation direction

Flanges

Web

Metal studs

If you built your walls with metal studs, the key consideration is the sequence of driving the screws. Instead of starting in the middle of the drywall's length, you begin at the end that has the open end of the flange. Another tip: Instead of aiming for the middle of the stud's flange, drive the fastener closer to the web (the metal part perpendicular to the wall). See *page 46* for more advice on working with metal studs.

**3** Slide the next panel into position, butting it very lightly against the first. Again, drive screws every 6 inches into the center wood strip. Drive a couple of screws through the adjacent panel into the wood strip. In this case, you're not trying to bend the drywall; you're merely anchoring the assembly to the rest of the wall.

**4** This overhead view through a butt joint illustrates how the back blocker curves the drywall into the stud cavity. Creating this recess makes it much easier to disguise the butt joint. The straightedge across the drywall shows how the back blocker pulled on the drywall ends.

## Back blockers

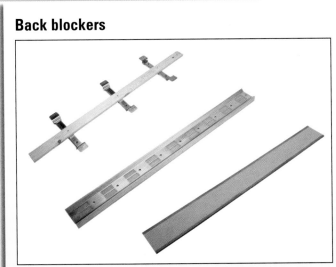

Ingenious designers have created a number of back blocker products. Despite differences in appearance, they share the same function of curving panel ends to make butt joints disappear. Some people prefer wider back blockers, figuring that the gentler curve creates less stress in the drywall.

**WHAT IF...**
## You can't find commercially made back blockers?

The solution is easy: Make your own. Simply rip 10-inch-wide strips of ¾-inch plywood 48 inches long. Top each edge with a ¾-inch-wide strip of ⅛-inch hardboard that you attach with ½-inch brads or staples.

The homebuilt version produces the same result as its commercial counterpart. Fastening the ends of the butt joint to the centerline of the plywood creates a slight concavity that's easy to tape and conceal.

# GYPSUM AND CEMENTIOUS BACKERBOARD

The introduction of backerboard products has made tile installation a more accessible project for the do-it-yourselfer. In the world before backerboard, the first step in a tile job was installing a mortar bed to provide structural rigidity so that the installed tiles couldn't flex and crack. Laying a smooth bed was a job that required the skilled touch of an experienced craftsman.

But just as drywall panels have made wall and ceiling installation less demanding than plastering, backerboard makes tile prep a job that doesn't require an apprenticeship.

Consult with several tile suppliers for recommendations on the best backerboard for your project. But be aware that the dealer's inventory may color the advice. For example, a supplier who stocks only cementious backerboard probably won't recommend gypsum panels, even though they are easier to cut.

## PRESTART CHECKLIST

☐ **TIME**
Approximately 20 minutes per panel

☐ **TOOLS**
Tape measure, drywall T-square, rasp, mixer, margin trowel, notched trowel for floor application; cut gypsum panels with a utility knife and use a standard holesaw for small holes, use a carbide scriber or abrasive wheel for cementious panels, use a carbide-tipped holesaw for small holes

☐ **SKILLS**
Measuring, marking, cutting, driving screws

☐ **PREP**
Gather tools and materials at job site

☐ **MATERIALS**
Backerboard, corrosion-resistant screws, compatible fiberglass mesh tape

## Gypsum backerboard

**1** Gypsum backerboard is easy to cut and shape. For straight cuts, you simply use a sharp utility knife to score, snap, and cut just as you do with gypsum wallboard. A jab saw makes internal cutouts.

**2** Be aware that the board has a face side that's a different color than the back. Follow the manufacturer's directions for adhering the board in a thinset bed. Backerboard requires special screws, so don't substitute ordinary drywall fasteners. Follow the fastener spacing recommended by the manufacturer.

## Cutting small holes

**1** Set the board against the pipe or other obstruction. Mark the diameter of the hole to be cut. Use a tape measure to locate the center of the hole. For faucets, measure the location of each faucet hole from the wall and from the tub or floor.

**2** Use a cordless drill and carbide-tipped hole saw or coring saw to cut small holes in backerboard. Place the drill point of the saw on the mark you made, and use light pressure and high speed to cut through the backerboard.

# Cementious backerboard

**1** When you're working with cementious backerboard, use a carbide scriber for the initial scoring. Make several passes with firm pressure.

**2** After you snap the board, keep the cut open at an angle while you slice with your utility knife. It will probably take several passes to separate the pieces. Smooth the cut edges with a rasp.

## Cutting large holes

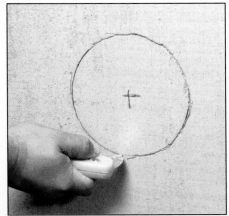

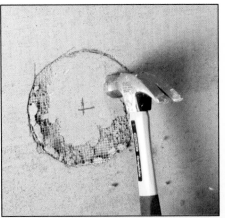

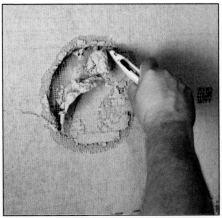

**1** When the diameter of a hole to be cut exceeds the size of available hole saws, measure the obstruction and use a compass to mark its location on the backerboard. Then score completely through the backerboard mesh with a utility knife or carbide scriber.

**2** Support the cutout with the palm of one hand, if necessary, and tap the scored edge with a hammer. Continue tapping until the surface around the circumference crumbles. Alternatively, drill a series of small holes around the circumference.

**3** Using a utility knife, cut through the mesh on the opposite side of the board. Push the cutout through and smooth the edges with a rasp, serrated contour plane, or masonry stone.

# TAPING, JOINT COMPOUNDS, & SANDING

This chapter begins after you've driven the last fastener to hang the final sheet of drywall in your project. On these pages, you'll receive basic training on several key phases: installing corner beads, spreading compound, sanding, and checking your work. You'll learn how to handle situations that are typical in nearly every drywalling project as well as some special tasks, including beading and mudding an archway.

## Making compounds less complex

Going to the hardware store or home center to get some joint compound can turn into a confusing expedition. Do you choose setting-type or premixed? Topping mix or all-purpose? No need to panic. This chapter describes the various types and makes clear recommendations.

By using the right compounds, you'll minimize downtime waiting for drying and create a smooth surface that's easy to sand. You'll also learn how to avoid common mistakes that could result in bulged butt joints or cracked seams.

## Beads and bullnose

Corner beads—either square or bullnose—protect outside corners from impact damage and also make a transition from one plane to another. Take your time with the first beads you install, and you'll get great results right from the start. As you gain a little experience with straight runs, you'll then learn how to make two- and three-way corners, such as those you often see in soffit corners above kitchen cabinets.

Bullnose two- and three-way corners may look complicated to the beginner, but vinyl and metal caps remove much of the hard work.

## Taping, mudding, and sanding

Before you start slapping on tape and mud, it's a good idea to have a definite sequence of the steps in mind. That way, you'll preserve reference surfaces to guide your drywall knife in the initial stages. You should have goals for each coat of compound; that way, you'll maximize productivity and minimize frustration. And when the dust clears after the sanding, you'll have walls and ceilings that are smooth, flat, and ready for paint.

---

## A little help and a lot of patience are the keys to professional quality drywall taping and finishing.

### CHAPTER PREVIEW

**Preparing Joint Compound**
*page 90*

**Working with fiberglass tape**
*page 92*

**Applying compound to a tapered seam**
*page 94*

**Corner beads**
*page 98*

*Covering fastener heads is one of the quickest and easiest parts of drywall finishing. Taping seams and installing corner beads take more time and practice, but you'll gain experience quickly. Top quality finishes are well within the reach of any do-it-yourselfer.*

**Two- and three-way corners**
*page 100*

**Installing bead in an archway**
*page 102*

**Sanding**
*page 104*

**Skim coating**
*page 106*

**Levels of finish**
*page 107*

# PREPARING JOINT COMPOUND

Setting-type compounds are an excellent choice for the first coat. Even with the relatively thick application needed to fill cracks and embed tape, you won't have to wait for evaporation before you move to the second coat. This can be an enormous advantage when you're working in humid weather. In addition, setting compounds provide more strength to the joints.

On the down side, setting compounds can be cumbersome to mix, and they have a restricted working time. Once the compound starts to set, you must react quickly to clean your tools and trash any unused material.

Premixed compounds are also often called ready-to-use. But more accurately, they are nearly-ready-to-use. At least once a day, redistribute the moisture within the bucket with a mudmasher. Otherwise the water migrates to the top, leaving the compound at the bottom of the bucket too stiff for easy spreading.

Keep the bucket of premixed compound tightly sealed when you aren't removing material. A snug lid keeps the moisture from evaporating while excluding dust and other contaminants from the bucket.

## PRESTART CHECKLIST

☐ **TIME**
About 5 or fewer minutes per batch

☐ **TOOLS**
Mixing bucket, kitchen scale, measuring containers, ½-inch drill with mixing paddle, mudmasher (for premixed compounds)

☐ **SKILLS**
Measuring and mixing

☐ **PREP**
All drywall panels are hung, scrap material removed, floor is clean, drywall knifes, mud pan, and tape are at hand

☐ **MATERIALS**
Setting-type compound, drinking-grade water

**1** If you're a first-time user of setting-type compound, carefully measure the ingredients until you acquire a feel for the correct consistency. Start with a clean mixing bucket, and pour in the amount of drinking-grade cool water you need for the batch size you're mixing. Weigh the compound, and gently sprinkle it into the water to avoid splashing.

**2** Chuck a mixing paddle into your drill, and stir the compound until you've removed all lumps. Keep the drill at a low speed—you want to stir, not whip air bubbles into the mix. Hold the bucket between your feet so that it doesn't spin. To make certain that there aren't any pockets of powder, scrape the sides and bottom of the bucket with a piece of scrap wood. Clean the mixer immediately so the compound doesn't harden on it.

## Applying compound

Before you apply the first coat of compound, install all of the metal or vinyl corner beads *(page 98)*. Inspect the drywall by pushing each panel firmly in several locations. If there's any movement or sound, drive additional fasteners. You'll also need to pre-fill any gaps over ¼ inch and repair any damage that occurred during installation.

**First coat** (use setting-type compound or all-purpose ready-mixed compound)
■ Apply self-adhesive fiberglass tape to tapered seams, butt seams, and inside corners. (If you use paper tape, you'll embed it in the first coat of compound.)
■ Apply compound to tapered seams.
■ Apply compound to butt seams.
■ Apply compound to outside corners.
■ Apply compound over fasteners.
**Second coat** (use setting-type compound or all-purpose ready-mixed compound)
■ Apply compound in same sequence as for first coat
**Third coat** (use all-purpose or topping ready-mixed compound, or an easy-sand setting-type compound)
■ Apply compound in same sequence as for first coat

**3** Loosen ready-mixed joint compound with a manual mudmasher. Moisture tends to migrate upward in ready-mixed containers—sometimes you'll even see a layer of water on the top. A few up and down strokes will help return the product to a uniform consistency. Avoid overmixing or power mixers because you'll whip bubbles into the compound, and they cause finishing problems. Discard the compound if there's any mold growth or it has an unpleasant odor.

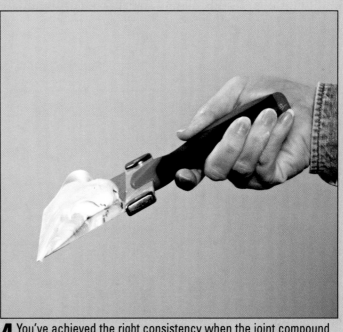

**4** You've achieved the right consistency when the joint compound doesn't slump under its own weight or readily slide off a taping knife held at a 45-degree angle.

## REFRESHER COURSE
### Setting vs. ready-mixed compounds

Setting-type and ready-mixed joint compounds produce similar results but achieve them in different ways. Understanding these processes will help you select the right compound—or combination of products—for your job.

Ready-mixed joint compound hardens as the water in it evaporates. You cannot apply a second coat until the first is thoroughly dry. With an all-purpose compound, you usually have to allow overnight drying for the relatively thick initial coat. If you try to accelerate drying by applying heat or pointing a fan directly at it, you invite trouble. Under those circumstances, the surface can dry before moisture escapes from below, and a crack is the usual result.

A setting-type compound is a powder that you add to water. In this case, the addition of moisture begins an irreversible chemical reaction that causes one of the ingredients, plaster of Paris, to harden. The precise proportions of other components in the compound determine how long the mix stays workable. As you can see in the accompanying chart, grade 20 compound, for example, has a total working time of 10 to 20 minutes. Once the chemical reaction reaches a certain point, the compound becomes progressively difficult to spread until it's unworkable. Don't try to add more water to the mix to extend working time—it simply won't work.

The setting time in the chart tells you the approximate time required until the compound has set enough to be recoated. Again using grade 20 as an example, you could apply a second coat about 20 minutes after you started mixing the first batch.

Fast-setting compounds are a great choice for prefilling (see *page 92*) or patches but can be difficult to manage for large-scale work. If you choose a compound with a longer setting time you'll have more working time for each batch but still have a setting time that's fast enough for you to apply two or more coats in a single day.

If you utilize setting-type compound for the first and second coats, you take advantage of their speed and strength. Use a ready-mixed topping compound for the third coat, and you'll enjoy its advantages of easy workability and sanding. Using a pair of products is called a two-compound system.

| GRADE | WORKING TIME (MIN.) | SETTING TIME (MIN.) |
|---|---|---|
| 15 | 7-12 | 10-18 |
| 20 | 10-20 | 15-25 |
| 30 | 15-30 | 25-40 |
| 45 | 25-50 | 40-55 |
| 60 | 40-80 | 55-85 |
| 90 | 60-110 | 85-115 |
| 120 | 100-140 | 115-160 |
| 210 | 150-220 | 180-240 |

# WORKING WITH FIBERGLASS TAPE

If you're a drywall novice, you'll find that fiberglass mesh tape is easier to use than paper tape. That's because paper tape needs to be pressed into layer of compound and the excess compound removed. The process is called embedding.

The trick is that you must remove surplus compound without wrinkling the tape or removing so much compound that the tape buckles because you've created dry spots. Faced with all of those paper tape challenges, you'll probably agree that fiberglass tape is worth its extra cost.

When you buy fiberglass tape, ensure that the package indicates that it's self-adhesive. While the non-adhesive version is relatively scarce, getting a roll could be an unpleasant surprise.

Be sure you keep a sharp utility knife blade available to cut fiberglass tape. A dull blade will merely skip over the fabric or snag the threads. If you're tackling a big project, consider the tape dispenser shown opposite. It's a speedy helper for both flat seams and inside corners.

**1** If you have gaps of ¼ inch or wider, you'll need to fill them before applying tape. Drywallers often call this process prefilling. Although you could utilize all-purpose ready-mixed compound for this step, the thick application can take a maddeningly long time to dry, delaying your project. For that reason, a setting-type compound with a short set time is your best choice.

**2** Repairing blowouts, miscuts, and other damage is the next step. In this case, careless handling during installation resulted in torn paper that reveals the gypsum core. Cover the damaged area with strips of fiberglass tape applied edge to edge. Cover the tape with a thin layer of compound. Again, a setting-type compound is a good choice for this step. Refer to *page 135* for information on fixing miscut electrical boxes and other repairs.

## PRESTART CHECKLIST

☐ **TIME**
Project time depends upon your experience level and the size of the room

☐ **TOOLS**
Mud pan, drywall knife, utility knife

☐ **SKILLS**
Cutting tape, spreading compound

☐ **PREP**
Compound is mixed and placed into the mud pan

☐ **MATERIALS**
Drywall compound, fiberglass mesh tape

### REFRESHER COURSE
### The three-coat system

Before you start slapping drywall compound onto your walls and ceilings, it's helpful to have a clear idea of what you're trying to accomplish with each application. Experienced drywallers produce a smooth surface in three coats, but beginners should prepare themselves for at least four coats.

One of the key problems is that drywall compound shrinks as it dries. So even if you achieve a flawless surface off your drywall knife, evaporation will create a depression as the compound dries.

On the first coat, you want to embed the tape at all joints and begin to fill the fastener holes. At outside corners, your goal is to begin a smooth transition from the outside edge onto the surface of the wall.

During the second coat, you'll fill the valley of tapered seams and feather the edges past the edges. At butt joints, you'll feather the

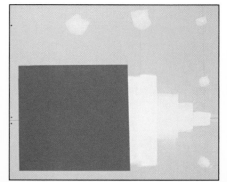

application outward in both directions from the seam. You'll also widen the application at inside and outside corners. A second coat over fasteners may nearly finish hiding them.

At the third coat, you continue to widen the application at every seam, corner, and over fasteners to create gradual transitions. You'll slightly overfill all areas to compensate for shrinkage and to create a small amount of surplus for sanding to a perfect surface.

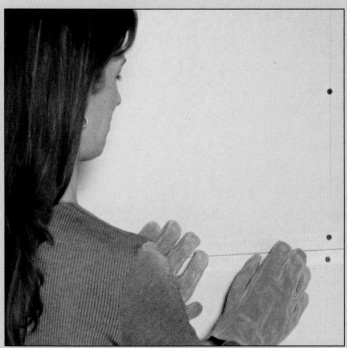

**3** Applying fiberglass tape by hand is extremely easy. Center its width over the centerline of the drywall seam, and press down firmly. Wearing a glove on your press-down hand protects your fingertips from abrasion. Cut the tape with a sharp utility knife. Apply the tape into tapered seams first, ending each wall with a cut at inside or outside corners.

**4** Use a 6-inch taping knife to shove fiberglass tape into inside corners, then press down both sides firmly. For maximum joint strength, keep the mesh centered in the corner. Run this layer of tape over the pieces that you applied to the tapered seams.

---

**STANLEY** PRO TIP

### Mud immediately over tape

Fiberglass tape doesn't have an aggressive adhesive, so it's not wise to trust it any longer than necessary, especially on ceilings. As soon as you finish taping a room, proceed immediately to the first coat of compound to embed the tape.

### Fast-draw taping

For big jobs consider a tape gun specifically made for applying fiberglass drywall tape. A built-in cutter neatly snips the tape so you don't have carry a utility knife. The tool firmly presses the tape into place for additional holding strength.

### Bag tape to keep adhesive fresh

Extend the life of fiberglass drywall tape by storing it in a plastic bag. Resealable bags are convenient, but you can also recycle a bread bag with a twist tie for this job. Airtight storage helps keeps the adhesive fresh, and you'll also shield the tape from drywall dust, another culprit that reduces tackiness.

# TAPING SEAMS AND CORNERS

In theory, tapered seams are easy. All you need to do is fill the valley between the two sheets of drywall, and you're finished. Putting that theory into practice is relatively straightforward, even though you do need to build the thickness in three or more coats. But because each layer shrinks a bit as it dries, the process rewards planning. In the end, you'll sand the final application to create a flat transition between the sheets.

Resist the urge to excessively mound up the compound in an effort to speed the job. That's like the road repair crew that overfills trouble spots, turning chuckholes into chuckhills—hardly an improvement.

Instead, count on at least three applications. At that point, carefully check your progress by spanning a drywall knife blade across the joint. Look for daylight between the blade and the compound. If the joint's filled, you're ready to sand. If the blade rocks because the compound's too high, be prepared for a sanding ordeal.

## PRESTART CHECKLIST

☐ **TIME**
Project time depends upon your experience level, application care, and the size of the room

☐ **TOOLS**
Mud tray, drywall knife, utility knife

☐ **SKILLS**
Cutting tape, spreading compound

☐ **PREP**
Compound is mixed and placed into mud pan

☐ **MATERIALS**
Drywall compound, fiberglass mesh tape

## Finishing tapered seams

**1** Cover the tape with a coat of setting-type or all-purpose compound applied with a 6-inch drywall knife. Lay on enough compound to completely cover the tape, but so that you can still faintly see the texture of the mesh. Avoid the temptation of building a thick coat with this first pass—you'll simply invite cracks as a result of uneven drying.

**2** If you use ready-mixed compound, wait until the first coat dries thoroughly. With setting-type compound, refer to the chart on *page 91* for advice on when to begin the next coat. There's no need to sand between coats of compound. Lightly push the edge of a drywall knife along the wall to knock down ridges or blobs.

## Half full or half empty?

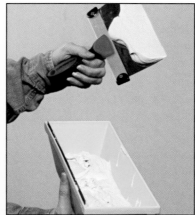

Whichever way you prefer to answer the philosophical question, fill your mud tray about halfway. If you're new to drywall, you'll be surprised how quickly a mud tray can seem heavy. There's no need to make the job more difficult than it needs to be.

## Loading the knife

Dip your drywall knife into the tray to load it, then scrape the back edge of the knife along the tray's edge to remove compound that clings there. Every few dips, scrape all the compound from the knife so that you don't get a line of compound that starts to dry on the knife. If you notice dried bits, scrape them into a disposal container.

**3** The purpose of the second coat is filling the tapered valley. Use a 10-inch drywall knife, and pull the compound along the seam to deposit material in a swath that matches the width of the knife. Again, avoid laying down too much material.

**4** For the third coat, switch to a 12- to 14-inch knife to complete the filling and to feather the compound onto the drywall. Stick with a 12-inch knife if you're a beginner—the 14-incher requires more skill to control.

## Feather the edges

Use a light touch when filling fastener holes or you won't leave enough material to allow for the inevitable shrinkage. Think about creating a feathered area all around the fastener's location instead of concentrating on filling only the dimple. A single stroke with a 6-inch knife covers fasteners on all three coats.

## Cover several holes in one stroke

You don't have to cover each fastener individually. Draw your knife over a row of fasteners at once and you'll speed your work. You'll also do a better job of disguising the location of the fasteners.

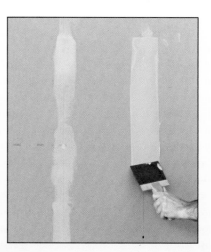

# Finishing butt joints

The long edges of drywall sheets are tapered. Two tapered edges together form a depression, which makes it possible to create a flat mud joint. The short edges of drywall sheets are not tapered; they meet at a butt joint.

Butt joints are more challenging to finish because they require that you build a slight, gradual mound to hide the joint. To make the mound subtle enough to go unnoticed, you must feather the joint compound over a wide area.

The same fiberglass mesh tape and similar techniques for applying mud are used for butt joints and tapered edges.

Apply the second coat of compound to the vertical butt seam after you've completed the second coat on the horizontal tapered seams, as shown in Step 2. That way, you'll do a better job of blending the intersection.

To minimize the difficulties of concealing butt joints, consider using a back blocking technique when hanging the drywall. See page 84 for more information.

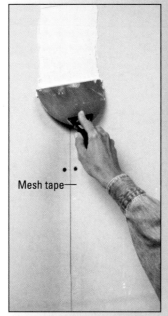

Mesh tape

**1** Cover the butt joint with fiberglass mesh tape. Use your 6-inch knife to cover the tape with mud.

**2** When the first coat of mud is dry, apply the second coat along both sides of the joint using a 6-inch drywall knife.

**3** Apply the third coat with a 12-inch drywall knife, feathering the edges out 8 to 10 inches on each side of the joint. You may leave a ridge down the center, but it can be scraped away later.

## Tapering the butt joint

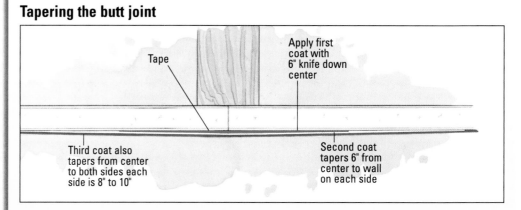

Tape

Apply first coat with 6" knife down center

Third coat also tapers from center to both sides each side is 8" to 10"

Second coat tapers 6" from center to wall on each side

The color-coded drawing gives you an idea of what you're trying to accomplish with each coat on a butt seam.

The first coat, indicated in blue, should be as thin as possible over the tape. If you use fiberglass mesh tape, it's fine if you still see the texture through the compound. Use the center of this seam as the reference line to feather the second and third coats further outward on the wall. You want to deposit as little compound as possible along the centerline. Concentrate on feathering outward from the center.

Apply the second coat (white) with a 6-inch knife. Make a 6-inch swipe to both sides of the joint's centerline.

You'll apply the third coat (coded red) with a 12-inch knife. Feather 8 to 10 inches outward from the centerline.

# Finishing corners

**C**overing corner bead at outside corners is easy because the bead itself guides the drywall knife. Run one side of your knife along the bead to produce a smooth, flat joint as the mud covers the nailing flange. As with other joints, apply at least three coats, sanding in between to feather the joint where it meets the drywall. The bead itself isn't hidden in mud. Simply scrape excess mud off the bead, then paint it along with the drywall.

Inside corners are more difficult. They require taping and mudding. The hard part is smoothing the mud on one side of the corner without messing up the mud on the other side.

Resist the temptation to try to get these inside joints perfect on the first, or even second, coat. Accept that there will be ridges you'll need to sand or knock off in the first two coats. To avoid ridges on the third coat, think of it as a filler coat; press hard on the knife so you fill imperfections instead of leaving behind a thick layer of joint compound. Remember there's no law against going over the joints a fourth time if necessary for a smooth finish.

## Finishing inside corners

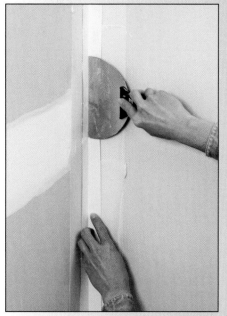

**1** Apply mud to both sides of the corner. Fold a length of paper tape in half (it is precreased) and press it into the mud with a 6-inch knife. An inside corner tool *(page 36)* embeds the tape and smoothes the joint on both sides at the same time.

**2** Embed the tape in the mud by drawing down the knife along both sides of the corner. Repeat this process to apply additional coats of mud. Sand to smooth the final surface.

## Check the butt joint

Use the edge of a 12-inch knife to check your progress in tapering a butt joint. With the middle of the blade at the centerline of the seam, an ideal seam will be nearly flat over the full length of the blade. If you see light between the blade and the wall or if the blade rocks more than $\frac{1}{16}$ inch in either direction, apply another coat. Again, taper from the centerline toward each side.

## WHAT IF...
### You find bubbles under the paper tape?

If there are bubbles under the tape, the tape doesn't stick to the mud, or it wrinkles, peel it off and apply more mud underneath. This is one time when applying a little too much mud is not a problem.

## Composite tape

If you're a beginner, you'll probably find that composite drywall tape will give you much faster and better results than paper tape at inside corners. You simply unroll the length you need, cut it with a knife, and fold it down the middle. Embedding is similar to working with paper tape, but the next coats are much easier because the stiff material creates a sharp inside corner. So instead of shaping the corner, you simply feather the compound away from it until you've concealed the tape's edges.

# CORNER BEADS

Most experts agree that installing corner beads and mudding them is one of the easier parts of the drywall process.

When you install beads, apply light pressure on the bead itself toward the corner. That will help ensure that the strip registers evenly along both walls and runs in a straight line. Misalignment can make the bead twist up the corner, and your only remedy is to rip it off and try again.

A quick tip: Always buy one or two spare beads for each one that you calculate you'll absolutely need. That will give you some backup material in the event a strip gets accidentally bent or if a miter is miscut.

Mudding beads is relatively easy because you have the corner to guide one edge of your knife as you spread the compound. Avoid excessive pressure because that will curve the blade of your knife, resulting in an underfilled concave corner.

## PRESTART CHECKLIST

☐ **TIME**
Project time depends upon the amount of bead that's required and the number of corners that must be fitted. Plan on 15 minutes to install one bead and fill the first coat of drywall compound.

☐ **TOOLS**
For metal or vinyl beads, you'll need tin snips; for composite bead, you'll need scissors or a utility knife

☐ **SKILLS**
Cutting bead stock, applying joint compound

☐ **PREP**
Drywall is hung; outside corners have no projections

☐ **MATERIALS**
Corner bead, ringshank drywall nails or corner clincher; if you use bullnose bead, you may need transition pieces to square off the corners at the top and bottom.

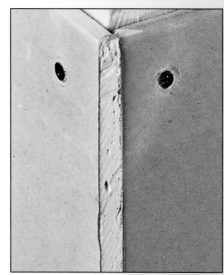

**1** At an outside corner, lap one sheet of drywall over the other and fasten it to the stud. Make sure that the end of the lapped sheet doesn't extend past the face of the other wall. If it does, rasp away the excess material. You don't have to achieve a perfect junction because the corner bead establishes the finished corner.

**2** Cut the corner bead to length with tin snips, keeping its bottom end about ½ inch off the floor. (Baseboard molding will conceal any gap at that end.) Lightly press on the corner of the bead, squaring the legs of the strip against the walls. Drive a few nails through the holes in the metal strip to establish its position, then nail through the metal for a more secure hold. Don't twist the bead or press it too tightly as you install it. Space the nails about 8 inches apart along each leg; make sure they are seated firmly.

### Clinch the bead

A corner bead clincher helps you squarely position the metal strip and then quickly fasten it. Each time you hit the clinching tool, it cuts prongs of metal and forces them into the drywall. For added security, drive three nails through each leg of the corner bead to establish a mechanical connection with the framing.

### Installing bullnose bead

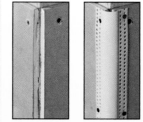

**1** With bullnose bead, you may need to install the drywall sheets so that they terminate flush with the corner of the framing. This placement is sometimes necessary to create clearance for the inside radius of the strip. Purchase bullnose bead strips before you hang the drywall to determine the proper corner treatment.

**2** Nail the metal or vinyl bullnose bead into place, spacing the fasteners about 8 inches apart along each leg. If your outside corner is significantly larger or smaller than 90 degrees, ask a drywall supplier about the availability of off-angle bullnose beads. Make sure the materials you'll need to execute your design are available before you begin work. Composite materials can adapt to square or off-angle applications.

**3** Use a 6-inch drywall knife to apply the first coat of compound to the corner. The blade of the knife glides along the raised bead and the wall, laying the mud into the valley between these two high points. Don't try to build too much thickness with this first coat or you'll risk cracking. Note that filling the tapered seam first gives the knife a continuous bearing surface across the joint.

**4** For the second coat, choose a 10-inch knife, and again bridge between the metal corner and the surface of the wall. Feather the compound along the wall to create a smooth transition. Use a 12-inch knife for the third coat to feather the compound even further onto the wall.

## Transition from bullnose to square

Bullnose corners add style and interest to your installation, but they can also create problems when you install millwork. For example, turning an outside corner with baseboards or crown moldings could call for fancy carpentry skills and tedious fabrication. Fortunately, there's a solution that you can simply nail in place when you're installing the bullnose bead. The vinyl 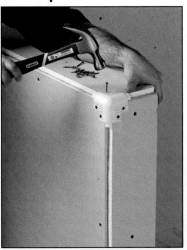 cap shown works with both metal and vinyl beads that have a ¾-inch radius and enables you to install moldings up to 4½ inches wide. Simply nail the blocks where you need them, and cut the strip of bullnose bead to fit. For a perfect size match, get both the bullnose bead and transition cap from a single manufacturer.

## Vinyl vs. metal vs. composite

To many traditionalists, vinyl is another word for plastic, and plastic is a synonym for cheap and brittle. But modern plastics technology produces high-performance materials that warrant careful consideration. For example, an abuse-resistant vinyl corner bead might be the right choice for high-traffic corners where impact is 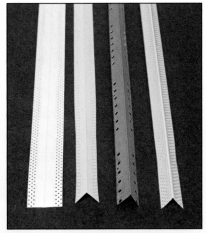 inevitable. If you've ever dented metal corner bead with a misplaced hammer blow during construction, you know that replacement is the only practical choice. Composite corner beads are also impact resistant and have the added benefit of conforming to corners that are substantially more or less than 90 degrees. If it isn't 90 degrees, a drywall pro calls it an "off angle."

# TWO- AND THREE-WAY CORNERS

You'll find two-way corners at doorways without wood trim and the inside corners of soffits. The outside corner of a soffit is a typical location for a three-way corner.

No matter where they're located, it's a good idea to invest some patience and extra care into the creation of these corners. A sloppy installation will raise the degree of difficulty in applying the drywall compound and can result in a misshapen corner that acts like a magnet for a visitor's eyes. But a carefully fitted corner will make mudding an easy task, and you'll be rewarded with crisp lines that generate compliments for your workmanship.

Bullnose corners are even easier than square profiles. That's because you can purchase vinyl and metal corner caps that make the installation extremely simple. You fit the caps first, then simply make square cuts at the ends of straight runs of bullnose stock to butt them into the preformed corners. It's a good idea to purchase the corners and bullnose stock from a single supplier to ensure that the radii are equal.

## PRESTART CHECKLIST

☐ **TIME**
Project time depends upon the amount of bead that's required and the number of corners that must be fitted. Plan on 15 minutes for the first bullnose strip.

☐ **TOOLS**
Tape measure, tin snips, file

☐ **SKILLS**
Accurate measuring and cutting

☐ **PREP**
Drywall is hung

☐ **MATERIALS**
Corner beads; preformed corners for bullnose application, ringshank drywall nails

## Two-way corner

**1** Before you install strips of metal corner bead at a corner, make a mitering nip at the end of each piece using tin snips. Otherwise the two thicknesses of metal will overlap at the corner. The miters don't have to fit perfectly—you simply want to avoid overlap.

**2** Nail the first strip into position, driving ring-shank nails right through the metal. Hammer squarely to avoid twisting the metal. Carefully position the second piece of corner bead to ensure that its tip neatly continues the line around the corner.

## Inside bullnose corners

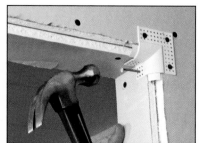

It's possible to miter bullnose corner bead, but you'd probably have a tough time getting the joint to align precisely. Skip the problem and get better results by purchasing two-way corner caps. The one shown is vinyl, but they are also manufactured in metal. You simply nail these caps into corners and connect them with square-cut lengths of bullnose bead. Some sample installation sites include door and window frames, closets, passageways, and skylights.

## Not too thick!

Bullnose corners can require substantial amounts of drywall compound to blend the bead into the walls. Avoid problems by choosing setting-type compound for the first coat or two, and resist the urge to apply it too thickly.

Instead of saving time, a too-heavy application strategy can backfire by cracking. To ensure that the crack won't telegraph through the final application, cover it with fiberglass or paper tape before applying the next coat of compound.

# Three-way corner

**1** If you build a soffit, you may have to deal with a three-way corner. After you cover the framing with drywall, double-miter a piece of corner bead for the long horizontal run, and nail it in place. Cut a double miter on another piece of bead, and then square-cut it to length for the other horizontal run. Match the tips of the two pieces as closely as possible.

**2** For the third piece of corner bead, you'll double-miter another piece for the vertical corner. Again, carefully fit its tip against the two that are already in position. After the third piece is in place, you may need to file the tips to correct any small misalignment. Finally, take a few file strokes across the point, slightly blunting it so that it's not dangerously sharp.

## Bullnose corner

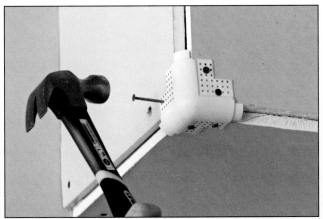

If you'd like to build a soffit with bullnose edges but are unsure how to tackle the three-way corners, the solution is much easier than you might think—a three-way cap is a quick and effective solution. Choose from metal or vinyl, and between ¾- and 1½-inch sizes. Take your time when you install the bullnose beads and cap to get a snug fit between the trim pieces and so that the lines are true and square.

## Three-way off-angle corner

If you were happy to discover that there's a corner cap for a three-way bullnose joint, you'll be even more delighted to find out that you also can purchase a cap for an off-angle corner. That way, you don't have to be limited to soffits and other constructions 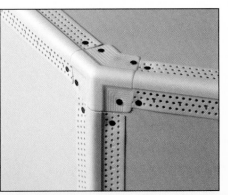 with square ends where they meet the walls. Instead, utilize a 135-degree end to make a gentler transition. At a drywall contractor's supply, you'll find these caps in metal and vinyl, and you can choose between bullnose radii of ¾ and 1½ inch.

# INSTALLING BEAD IN AN ARCHWAY

**A**n archway is a classic architectural design element that can add character to your home and speak about your good taste.

Flank the archway with fluted columns topped with ornate capitals, and you'll give a room a stunning Greek neoclassical flair. A simple archway with a stucco texture on the walls can evoke an Italian villa, a Mexican hacienda, or California's Spanish Revival architecture. With smooth walls and sleek transitions, the look is thoroughly modern. So no matter what design vocabulary you speak, an archway will help you make a fluent statement.

Modern innovations in materials have made archways easier than ever to build and finish. Refer to the framing instructions that begin on *page 54,* and you'll discover that creating the curves is a straightforward process. And installing the bead isn't difficult when you follow the procedure on these pages.

Many archways eliminate wood trim, so you avoid the lumber expense and skip an exacting carpentry chore.

## PRESTART CHECKLIST

☐ **TIME**
Project time depends on the size of the archway. Plan on 2 hours to apply the trim on a 6-foot-wide arched doorway and apply the first coat of compound.

☐ **TOOLS**
Utility knife, drywall mud tray, knives

☐ **SKILLS**
Embedding drywall tape, installing corner bead

☐ **PREP**
Opening is framed and drywall is hung

☐ **MATERIALS**
Composite arch tape, metal corner bead, drywall compound

**1** Install corner bead along both vertical legs of the arched opening, but stop the metal at least 2 inches below the start of the curve. Unroll composite archway beading against the inner curve of the archway to roughly fit the length. Add 3 or 4 inches, and cut the tape with scissors. Cut another piece of tape to the same length for the other side of the archway.

**2** Fold the tape in half lengthwise along its crease, pressing the printed sides together. An inexpensive metal folding tool makes this a quick process. If you don't have the folding tool, wear gloves to protect your fingers from abrasion.

## WHAT IF...
### You want a bullnose archway?

You can find vinyl and metal bullnose beading that has a notched flange so that you bend it to fit your archway. The maximum length of this material is 10 feet, so you won't be able to go from floor to floor with a single piece. Splicing in the middle of a curved run would be difficult, so your best bet is to cover the curved portion with a single piece, as shown in the drawing. It's then a simple matter to attach straight lengths of bullnose beading from the curve to the floor. Fasten both the curved and straight portions with drywall nails driven into the framing.

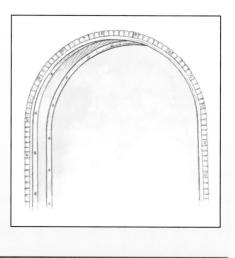

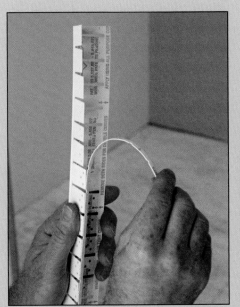

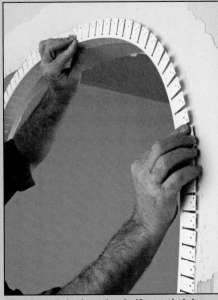

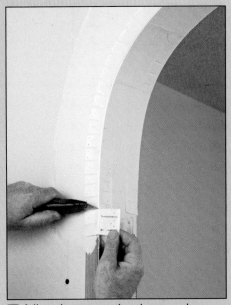

**3** To get the beading to follow the archway, you'll remove the strip along one edge to allow the notches to expand along the flat wall. Fold the edge of the strip back against the tape to crease it, and then zip it for a clean separation.

**4** With a 6-inch taping knife, apply joint compound to the inside of the archway and the flat wall. Starting at the center, press the tape firmly into the compound. Work around the archway until the tape overlaps the corner bead at both ends.

**5** Adjust the tape so that the curve is smooth. When you're satisfied with the result, wipe away excess joint compound. Finally, cut the tape to length so that its tip exactly meets the end of the metal bead. You can apply another coat of compound immediately, provided you avoid excessive thickness. After that application sets, apply one or two coats of compound, then sand.

---

 PRO TIP

### Bead can eliminate trimwork

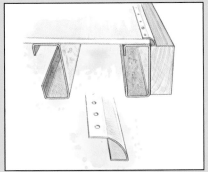

For a clean, modern look—or simply to eliminate the labor and expense of wood trimwork—consider using J- or L-beads at doorways and other openings. The metal J-bead in the drawings has a bullnose profile that makes a softer transition than the usual squared-off J-bead profile.

### WHAT IF...
### You have to run drywall up against a post or other surface?

When a raw drywall edge meets a dissimilar surface, such as wood, it is nearly impossible to get a clean fit. Two products create a crisp edge in this situation. J-bead is nailed into the wall before the drywall is installed. Prepaint it because it remains visible when the job is finished. (Spray paint works well.) J-bead is particularly useful where condensation might wick into the drywall. It encases the drywall, isolating it from the abutting material. L-bead is nailed to the face of the drywall. It is covered with joint compound (as corner bead is) after installation and painted with the rest of the wall. This bead does not extend over the back of the sheet.

# SANDING

Ask drywallers about the worst part of the job, and sanding will get a landslide number of votes. The fine dust clouds the air and migrates through the smallest crack to the farthest corners of your home. Forget to wear a cap, and your hair will feel like a day-old plate of spaghetti.

But no matter how evil the job seems, it's a necessary evil. You can minimize the dread by having the right equipment, suiting up properly, and searching out products that control dust at the source or prevent it from spreading to clean areas of your house.

Check *page 39* for vacuum accessories that suck up dust before it can become a nuisance and for a plastic wall barrier system that seals off your work area.

No matter how much you may dislike sanding, don't shortchange the process. If you don't give this part of the job your best effort, all of your other hard work will be ruined. Be patient, be persistent, and you'll be rewarded.

## PRESTART CHECKLIST

☐ **TIME**
Project time depends on the size of the room, the number of joints, and the skills of the person applying the compound

☐ **TOOLS**
Sanding pole, hand sanding block, bright light with extension cord, dust mask, safety glasses, cap, long drywall knife for inspection

☐ **SKILLS**
Sanding, checking your work

☐ **PREP**
Joint compound applied over all seams, fasteners, and beads

☐ **MATERIALS**
Sanding screen, drywall compound for touch-ups

**1** To load a sander, capture one end of a die-cut sheet of sanding screen under the clamping mechanism, making certain that the abrasive sheet is square to the holder. Smooth the screen over the pad and attach its end under the other clamp. Load a hand sander by resting it on a flat surface. With a pole sander, you can lean the pad against the wall while your foot keeps the pole from slipping. When the abrasive sheet loses its cutting power, turn over the screen to reveal a fresh surface.

**2** Knock down nubs and ridges with your 6-inch drywall knife to speed the sanding process. Set a box fan in an open window to exhaust fine airborne particles from the work site. A pair of bungee cords holds a furnace filter on the intake side of the fan. This setup captures most of the fine dust to maintain peace with your neighbors.

## Sponging to smooth a surface

After you apply the final coat of mud and it dries, the final step is to smooth the surface. You have two choices: sponging or sanding. Each method has its advantage. Sponging avoids creating dust, but sanding does a better job of making the joint flat.

To sponge, you'll need a bucket of water and a big sponge. Even better is a sponge made especially for smoothing drywall; it has a coarse mesh on one side that removes excess mud and a plain sponge on the opposite side for refining the surface. Wet the sponge and scrub the wall surface. Rinse the sponge frequently to get rid of the mud that builds up on its surface.

*Scrape off the ridges and lumps, then sponge the wall smooth. Be careful not to scrub too hard on the paper areas—you can actually wear away the paper and create a rough spot.*

**3** Take long strokes with the pole sander. The weight of the sanding head supplies enough pressure—bearing down on the tool will only make you tired. To remove sanding dust from the screen, slightly lift one end of the pad from the wall and tap it.

**4** Use a light touch when you work into corners. The sanding screen is slightly wider than the pad; the screen folds over the edge of the pad and smoothes part of the adjacent wall. But be careful that you don't create ruts in the corners or you'll have to apply more compound to cover your blunder.

**5** To really capture sanding dust, consider a sander that works with your shop vac to grab dust before it gets airborne. Some sanders have a hose that connects directly to a shop vac, requiring you to periodically clean its filter. Other sanders, like the one shown in the photo, have a water filter that grabs the dust before it reaches the vacuum's filter. The basic outfit includes the hand sander, and the pole sander is an optional accessory. (See Magna Industries on "Resources" *page 139.*)

---

**STANLEY** PRO TIP

### Tape identifies problem areas

Have a roll of masking tape handy when you're sanding so you can stick a small strip to the wall to mark an area that needs a little more joint compound. Wipe the sanding dust from the wall with your hand so that the tape will stick.

**STANLEY** PRO TIP

### Check the show coat

A work light held at a raking angle helps reveal ridges, bumps, and depressions as you scrape and sand between coats. But your best—and last—chance to fix finish flaws is after you have applied a primer coat—the show coat—to the walls. At this point the walls are a uniform color and you'll see irregularities you might not have noticed before priming. The most common beginner's mistake is joints that are too thick. If you find joints like this, add another coat of mud and feather it out farther. Sand these joints again, apply primer to any bare mud, and you are ready to apply paint once the primer dries.

### Folding abrasive screen

You'll get the flattest results by using a sanding block or pole sander whenever possible. But for the occasional tight area, fold a sheet of abrasive screen into thirds. Apply light pressure over as broad an area as possible. If you use heavy fingertip pressure, you can sand divots into your wall. Always think of sanding an area, not merely a spot.

# SKIM COATING

**1** Thin down the joint compound so that it's loose enough to apply with a paint roller but not so thin that it's runny. Put a metal paint roller screen into your 5-gallon bucket and you won't have to transfer the material to a tray. Roll a uniform coat onto a wall area of about 40 square feet.

**2** Use a wide drywall knife—12 to 14 inches—to immediately strike down the surface. You don't want to remove every bit of the compound, but you do want to leave a thin uniform coat with a minimum of tool marks. Deposit the removed material into your drywall tray, then dispose of it. Dumping it back into the bucket could contaminate the batch with dried bits and other impurities from the wall.

 PRO TIP

### On a roll

Buckets of drywall mud are heavy, and lugging them around your job site makes the job more difficult than it needs to be. Save your back by purchasing a four-wheel furniture dolly and topping it with a piece of plywood. The platform is large enough to support two 5-gallon buckets and makes a handy storage spot for tools.

### Cleaning up the work area

Promptly clean spilled or dripped compound from the floor for easiest removal. Keep a 4-inch plastic putty knife and a small cardboard box handy for this purpose. If the compound hardens, chip it off the subfloor with a long-handled ice scraper (as used on sidewalks) or with a flat shovel.

# LEVELS OF FINISH

Drywall installation and finishing is ultimately about achieving a suitable surface, and that may range from strictly utilitarian to high-end decorative.

For example, many contractors finish the walls of attached garages only enough to achieve the fire rating mandated by building codes. While the surface is serviceable, it's often far from smooth. At the other end of the spectrum is a dining room wall that will have glossy paint and will be illuminated by ceiling canisters close to the wall that rake light across it at a shallow angle. Under those critical conditions, even a tiny imperfection will draw attention.

So it's important that you finish your drywall with its end purpose in mind. Otherwise you waste time, energy, and money to achieve an unnecessarily smooth surface, or you risk disappointment with the final result by not investing enough into the project.

Understanding the various levels of finish is especially important if you hire someone to install or finish drywall. Terms like "industry standards" and "workmanlike finish" are vague and inadequate for contracts. That's why the Gypsum Association cooperated with several other trade organizations to draft a document that details the recommended levels of gypsum board finish. The following information summarizes that document, and you can contact the Gypsum Association for even more detailed information. (See "Resources" on *page 139*.)

## Level 0

This level requires no taping, finishing, or corner beads.

You might specify this level of work from a contractor when you're going to do the finishing. Another example is an area where no decisions have yet been made on the ultimate finish.

## Level 1

All interior angles and joints should have tape set into joint compound. The surface should be free of excess of joint compound. Ridges and tool marks are acceptable.

At this level, fasteners are not necessarily covered. In some municipalities, this level may be called "fire-taping" if it meets the code requirement for fire resistance. This level of finish is generally utilized for nonpublic areas of a building, such as a garage or attic.

## Level 2

At this level, all interior angles and joints should have tape embedded in joint compound and wiped with a trowel or joint knife, leaving a thin coating of compound. Fastener heads, corner beads, and other accessories are covered with a coat of joint compound. Ridges and tool marks are acceptable, but the surface should not have excess joint compound. If joint compound is applied over the tape when it is embedded, this is considered a separate coat of compound to satisfy the requirements of this level.

Level 2 is sometimes specified when water-resistant gypsum backing board is used as a substrate for tile. This level is sometimes specified for garages and other areas where appearance is not important.

## Level 3

All joints and interior angles should have tape that's embedded in joint compound plus one additional coat of joint compound. Accessories and the heads of fasteners must be covered with two separate coats of joint compound. All joint compound must be smooth and free of ridges and tool marks.

For Level 3 and above, the prepared surface should be coated with a drywall primer that's compatible with the wallcovering, paint, or other decoration being applied to it. The application of primers, however, is usually outside the responsibility of the drywall installer and finisher.

## Level 4

All joints and interior angles should have tape that's embedded in joint compound plus two separate coats of compound over all flat joints and one separate coat over interior angles. Accessories and fastener heads are covered with three separate coats of joint compound. All joint compound is smooth and free of ridges and tool marks.

Specify this level when you'll apply a light texture, wallcovering, or flat paints. Gloss and semigloss paints are not recommended over this level. The weight and texture of wallcoverings must be carefully considered to ensure that joints and fasteners will be adequately concealed. Wallcoverings that are lightweight, glossy, or have limited patterns are especially vulnerable to revealing imperfections in the surface.

## Level 5

At level 5, all joints and interior angles have tape that's embedded in joint compound plus two separate coats of compound over all flat joints and one separate coat over interior angles. Accessories and fastener heads are covered with three separate coats of joint compound. A thin skim coat of joint compound is applied over the entire surface. The surface should be smooth and free of ridges and tool marks.

This level represents the highest quality of finish, and it is the one recommended where gloss, semigloss, or nontextured flat paints are used or where severe lighting conditions exist. It provides the most uniform surface and minimizes the possibility of joints or fasteners showing through the finish.

This information is based on ASTM C 840-04, "Standard Specification for Application and Finishing of Gypsum Board." See "Resources" on *page 139* for contact information.

# ADVANCED DRYWALL TECHNIQUES

In magazines or on home tours, you may have seen spectacular drywall effects such as a curved wall, a barrel-vaulted ceiling, a ceiling that's paneled, or one that's stair-stepped. But features like these aren't reserved exclusively for upscale homes. All of these looks are well within the reach of the do-it-yourselfer. We've included plenty of tips and revealed some helpful professional tricks to help ensure your success.

## Looking up

In many ways, customizing a ceiling is easier than dealing with walls. That's because you don't need to work around multiple electrical boxes, baseboards, window and door jambs, and other millwork. And many times, you don't even need to demolish the old ceiling.

If you're building a coffered ceiling like the one on *page 112,* you can get building as soon as you clear the room. As long as the central portion of your ceiling is solid, you can leave it in place, although you may want to remove the texture. To see how to accomplish that, please check *page 133.*

## The raised panel look

Raised panel wainscots are another designer feature that you can build into your home. The job involves a little bit of planning and some careful installation work, but there really aren't any difficult procedures involved.

There are also raised panel designs suitable for upper walls, stairways, and ceilings. But don't try to cram all of these features into a single room—that would give it a choppy appearance.

## Bending the rules

Curved walls and barrel-vaulted ceilings can be spectacular, and they really aren't beyond your reach. We've included a chart that shows the minimum radii for a variety of drywall panels applied lengthwise, width-wise, wet and dry. The chapter "Framing for Drywall" provides the details you need.

## All access

Although access panels may sound mundane today, they're a handy feature when the shower valve starts leaking or a drain line is clogged.

If you're converting an attic, basement, or garage into extra living area, you'll be especially glad you discovered how easy it is to install access panels. The panels provide an easy solution to a number of utility problems.

## Special drywall features are well within the reach of a do-it-yourselfer.

### CHAPTER PREVIEW

**Bending drywall panels**
*page 110*

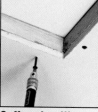

**Coffered ceiling**
*page 112*

**Raised panel drywall**
*page 114*

**Access panels**
*page 116*

An arched opening may look tricky at first glance, but it's really just a matter of following a series of easy steps.

# BENDING DRYWALL PANELS

**A** curved wall can create a true sense of motion within a room, and a barrel-vaulted ceiling can make a ho-hum hall into a pleasant passageway. Look around your house, and you may discover several opportunities for creating curves.

When you're planning the project, consult the chart below for the minimum radius that you can achieve with various thicknesses of drywall. If you must use ¼- or ⅜-inch panels, install at least two layers to make your finished wall a minimum of ½-inch thick. When you're framing the project, consult the chart on *page 45* to see the maximum stud spacing. Of course, you can place your studs closer together—that additional support will make your wall smoother and stronger.

One manufacturer cautions against wetting down the ¼-inch flexible panels to try to achieve a tighter curve—a crumbling panel is the likely result. You'll simply need to design your project within the bending limits of the panels.

Thin panels can be difficult to handle by yourself without damaging them, so it's a good idea to recruit a helper or two for this part of the project.

## PRE-START CHECKLIST

☐ **TIME**
Wetted panels require at least one hour of soaking time

☐ **TOOLS**
Drywall screws or nails

☐ **SKILLS**
Driving fasteners

☐ **PREP**
Wall is framed

☐ **MATERIALS**
Drywall panels in a thickness appropriate for the radius of your project

**1** Check the chart below to determine if you need to wet the drywall to make it flexible enough for the radius you're covering. Apply clean room-temperature water with a sponge, garden sprayer, or paint roller. Coat the face for application to an inward (concave) curve, and on the back for an outward (convex curve).

**2** Stack the wetted surfaces face-to-face, and give the water at least one hour to work. If the weather is extremely hot or dry, cover the stack with plastic sheeting so that water doesn't evaporate too quickly. Note that the panels rest on 2×4s atop the sawhorses so that they don't sag under their own weight.

## REQUIREMENTS FOR BENDING DRYWALL

| PANEL THICKNESS (INCHES) | MINIMUM RADIUS (INCHES); DRY, HORIZONTAL | MINIMUM RADIUS (INCHES); DRY; VERTICAL | MINIMUM RADIUS (INCHES); WET HORIZONTAL | WATER REQUIRED ON ONE SIDE (US FLUID OUNCES) |
|---|---|---|---|---|
| ¼ flexible | 32 | 45 | NR | NR |
| ¼ | 36 | 60 | 24 | 30 |
| ⅜ | 72 | 108 | 36 | 35 |
| ½ | 144 | NR | 48 | 45 |
| ⅝ | 216 | NR | NR | NR |

*Application direction refers to the position of the long edge of the drywall panel applied to a wall.*
*NR = not recommended*

**3** When you're applying drywall to an outside curve, start at one end stud and work toward the other end. Drive all the fasteners in each stud before moving to the next one. Let the ends run long, and trim them later.

**4** Start at the middle of an inside curve, and work toward both ends. Drive all the fasteners in each stud before moving to the next one. Let the ends run long, and trim them later.

**5** Trim the ends to length with the usual steps of score, snap, and cut. If you wet the drywall, you may want to wait until the board dries somewhat before cutting.

## Dealing with archways

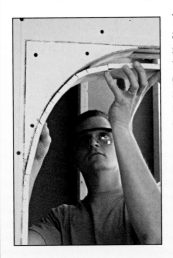

Treat the interior of an archway as you would a miniature wall— start in the center, and work toward the ends. Try this trick to get a tighter bending from a dry strip of ½-inch material. Cut the strip to width, then make crosswise scoring cuts spaced 1 inch apart on the back side. You may see small facets on the face of the drywall after you install it, but they'll disappear when you apply the joint compound.

## Allow drying time

Give the curved wall plenty of time to dry before you apply tape and joint compound. To gauge if the wall is dry, place your palm flat on the wall. If the surface feels cooler than the other walls in the room, it needs additional drying time.

# COFFERED CEILING

The coffered ceiling is adaptable to a variety of treatments by changing the number of steps and by adding moldings. You'll build each step from 2× lumber, which measures 1½ inches thick, plus a layer of ½-inch drywall. As a result, each step adds 2 inches of thickness.

A room with a standard 8-foot ceiling can easily tolerate a 2-inch loss of headroom in the name of style. A second layer in that room isn't out of the question. But if you want to add a third step, your original ceiling height should be at least 8 feet, 6 inches or higher to avoid a claustrophobic feeling.

The engineering is straightforward, as you can see in the section view drawings below. The two-step ceiling has a 2×4 strip above the second strip. This additional lumber width provides a nailing surface if you want to add moldings. Cove, crown, or bed moldings are three possibilities. The addition of moldings has two positive benefits: The millwork adds style and interest, and you don't need to be as precise with your drywall work when the inside corner is covered.

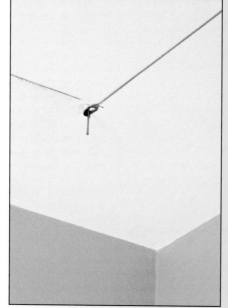

**1** Measure out the desired distance from the walls, and snap chalk lines to define the perimeter of the 2×2 framework. To make a step 16 inches wide, for example, snap the chalk lines 15½ inches from the walls to account for the thickness of the ½-inch drywall on the edge of the frame.

**2** Using your stud finder, mark the position of the ceiling joists. Make your lines right on the ceiling between the chalk lines and the walls, because the new drywall will cover that area. Attach the 2×2 strips to the ceiling with construction adhesive and screws driven into the joists. For the strips that run parallel to the joists, adopt one of the solutions explained in "What If" on the opposite page.

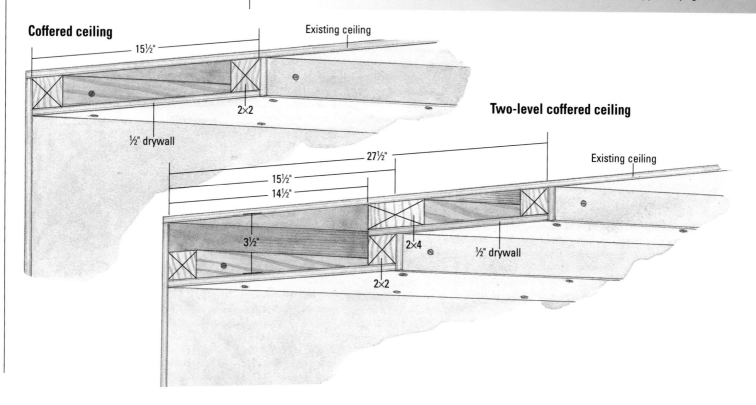

**Coffered ceiling**

15½"
Existing ceiling
2×2
½" drywall

**Two-level coffered ceiling**

27½"
15½"
14½"
3½"
2×4
½" drywall
2×2
Existing ceiling

**3** Screw or nail a 2×2 strip around the perimeter of the room where the walls and ceiling meet. Again, use construction adhesive and drive fasteners into the studs. Don't use a level to establish a perfectly flat plane for these strips—that will merely emphasize any out-of-level condition your ceiling currently has.

**4** Cover the framework with drywall, attaching it with construction adhesive and screws. Add a strip of drywall along the edge of the 2×2.

**5** Nail metal corner bead along the edges of the drywall, mitering the corners with tin snips for a neat fit. For best results, drive 1⅝-inch ringshank nails through the metal instead of through the holes punched in the metal. Add drywall tape to the inner corners and apply joint compound to the inside and outside corners. See *page 109* for tips and techniques.

## WHAT IF…
### There's no joist where you need to attach a strip?

At first, you might be tempted to simply attach the strip to the ceiling with construction adhesive and toggle bolts. But that's not a good idea because it makes the drywall on the ceiling support the load of the strip plus the weight of the drywall. Doing that would exceed the drywall's limits because it was not engineered to handle such an application.

The right approach is to add blocking between the joists so that the screws through the strips hit a solid anchoring point. This blocking can be 2× stock bridged between the joists or a continuous length of lumber added to the side of a joist. If you're redoing the entire ceiling in the room, add blocking while the joists are exposed. If you have access to an attic above the ceiling, you can add blocking without disturbing the existing

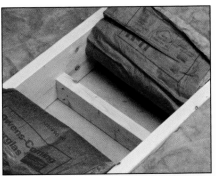

surface. As a last resort, you'll need to cut away the existing ceiling between joists to add the blocking. That's not as big a deal as it sounds, because you'll be adding drywall and spreading joint compound anyway. A little more area to cover is not a significant problem.

**STANLEY** PRO TIP

### Mitering corner bead

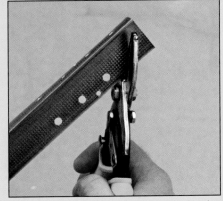

Before you install strips of metal corner bead along an inside corner, make a miter nip at the end of each piece with a pair of tin snips. Otherwise, you'd have the bulk of two thicknesses of metal overlapping at the corner.

# RAISED PANEL DRYWALL

A room decorated with raised panel walls or ceiling was always considered a sign of wealth. Besides the expense of the materials, the homeowner had to pay a skilled finish carpenter for the time-consuming and tedious work of fitting the framework and panels. But an innovative drywall product transforms this look into a do-it-yourself project with no fancy carpentry skills involved.

Although you'll probably need to special-order the panels, you'll find a variety of designs that work well as a wainscot treatment, as an upper-wall design, or even for ceiling application. You don't have to cover your entire wall or ceiling—you can center your design and fill in the edges with regular drywall panels.

Careful layout is essential, so invest the time needed to create some careful sketches of your project. The manufacturer's website (Pittcon Industries in "Resources" *page 139*) offers some helpful design suggestions.

As shown in the demonstration here, the easiest installation method involves using the decorative panels as the overlay in a two-thickness wall. If you're remodeling a room, you probably can skip the demolition phase.

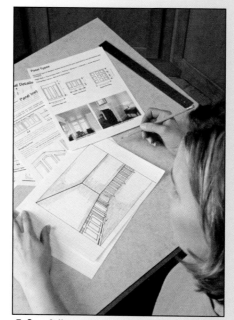

**1** Carefully measure your walls, and plan your layout. Don't feel that you need to cover every square inch with decorative panels—you can use ordinary drywall as filler strips and for flat wall surfaces.

**2** Transfer layout marks from your drawing to the room. Lines marked on the floor indicate the first panel's position, and nails driven into the sidewalls support a leveled nylon mason's line about ¾ inch away from the installation surface.

## PRESTART CHECKLIST

☐ **TIME**
Installation time depends upon the size and complexity of your project

☐ **TOOLS**
Chalk line, nylon mason's line, line level, caulking gun, hammer or drywall screwgun

☐ **SKILLS**
Leveling, accurate measuring and marking, driving fasteners

☐ **PREP**
Framing completed, first layer of drywall installed

☐ **MATERIALS**
Decorative panels and regular drywall, drywall panel adhesive, nails or screws

### WHAT IF...
### You want to add wainscot panels to an existing wall?

To add wainscoting, you don't necessarily need to start at bare studs. You can cap finished panels with a lip molding that simultaneously conceals the top edge and adds a decorative chair rail. A back band is a molding style that also hides the top edge but has a plain front profile.

**3** Untie one end of the level line so you can apply adhesive to the wall. Press the panel against the wall while a helper resets the level line. Level to the edge of the debossed pattern, not the edge of the panel itself. Drive screws to secure the panel.

**4** Repeat the process to install the next panel. This time you'll level the panels again, but you also need to measure between the edges of the pattern to maintain consistent spacing.

**5** Install all of the decorative panels, then fill in with flat drywall. Tape and finish the joints in the usual manner.

## Bend the design at the corner

The simplest solution at an inside corner is to end the last panel's design at least 4 inches from the corner. On the next wall, you start the design at an equal distance, and fill in with flat drywall. Be sure to allow for the thickness of the overlapped drywall at the corner so your layout is consistent.

It's also possible to make the design turn the corner. To do that, score the back of the panel with a sharp utility knife, taking care not to break through the front of the panel at the thin parts of the design. Gently snap the panel, then reinforce the corner with an thick bead of construction adhesive. Handle the panel carefully so you don't accidentally rip the face paper.

A drywall T-square helps you make the scoring cut on the back of the panel.

Reinforce the back of the corner with a bead of construction adhesive. Handle the panel with care and install it immediately.

# ACCESS PANELS

In a bathroom, an access panel is the no-demolition route to the back side of faucets, the drain for a bathtub, and the mixing valve of a shower. When it's time for repairs and replacements, access is literally a snap instead of adding hit-and-miss wall demolition and patching on top of the plumbing chores.

Access panels are particularly helpful when you're converting utility spaces like a basement, attic, or garage into a living area. By installing access panels, you preserve the ability to find and easily reach shut-off valves and drain cleanouts.

But you don't have to limit the panels to plumbing applications—you can also utilize them for easily reaching breaker boxes, electrical junction boxes, runs of telephone and data cable, plus other uses.

You can purchase metal and plastic access panels in a wide variety of sizes—from fist-sized to large enough to permit an average-sized person to crawl through. Some styles of purchased panels—like the ones shown here—permit a choice between easy surface mounting or flush mounting. You'll see that flush mounting is slightly more difficult but much less visible.

## PRESTART CHECKLIST

☐ **TIME**
Allow 20 minutes to install a small access panel

☐ **TOOLS**
Tape measure, level, jab saw, caulking gun

☐ **SKILLS**
Leveling, cutting an opening in drywall

☐ **PREP**
Identify location for panel

☐ **MATERIALS**
Purchased access panel, drywall panel adhesive

## Surface mounted panel

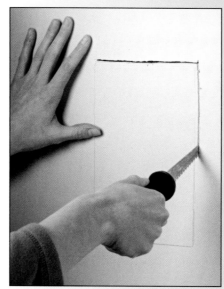 

**1** Surface-mounting an access panel is quick and easy. At the chosen spot, level the housing on the wall and trace its outline with a pencil. Using a jab saw, cut out the hole.

**2** Squirt a small bead of construction adhesive along the rear perimeter of the flange, and press the housing into place. The door simply snaps into position. If you paint the plastic the same color as the wall, caulk the edges of the housing to help blend it into the wall.

## Framed access panel

It's easy to build your own access panels. If the panel is hidden inside a closet, you may want to skip the wood frame and simply screw the drywall directly to the framing.

If you do make the frame, plan its size so that it will completely hide the edges of the drywall panel. For framing stock, you can select economical flat lumber or opt for a decorative molding.

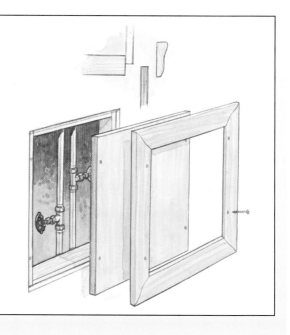

# Flush mounted panel

**1** Flush-mounting a plastic access panel begins with the same layout and cutting steps described in Step 1. To get the best fit, keep the edges of the cut square to the surface of the wall.

**2** For flush installation, the entire housing goes into the hole, and is held by construction adhesive between the flange and the back surface of the wall. Test-fit the housing before applying adhesive. The housing shown is designed for a flush fit in $\frac{5}{8}$-inch drywall. If your walls are thinner, add flat shims between the flange and drywall.

**3** Fill any cracks between the housing and the wall with drywall compound. Sand smooth, and paint the housing and panel to match your wall. The finished result is barely noticeable.

---

**STANLEY** Pro Tip: **Installing access panels in tight spots**

Tight clearances may make it impossible to install flush-mount access panels in some circumstances—you simply won't be able to get the housing completely through the hole. In new construction, you can install the housing before you hang the drywall. When you're remodeling, cut out an oversize rectangular piece of drywall, install the housing into it, then patch the piece back into the wall.

## Use clamps when gluing

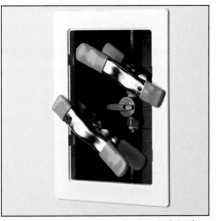

Inexpensive spring clamps do a great job of holding the plastic housing firmly against the wall until the construction adhesive sets. Clamping the housing lets you continue with other tasks without fear that you'll accidentally knock it out of position.

# DECORATIVE FINISHES & SPECIAL FINISHES

The primary objective of framing, drywall hanging, and finishing is the production of smooth surfaces—plumb walls and flat ceilings where neither your hand nor eye detects a single seam or fastener.

But many people find that such perfect surfaces are a bit boring. Some homeowners simply can't resist the temptation to create textures, install a medallion, or apply stenciled decorations. And even those who can resist all of those urges will hang shelves, pictures, and mirrors on their walls.

### Richly textured
Ceilings are a favorite target for textures. Contractors love spraying them with a texture called "popcorn" or "cottage cheese." Although the contractor's primary motivation is to boost his profit by skipping the work of sanding the ceiling, the texture does have a decorative purpose as well.

If you want to texture your walls, you can choose from an enormous spectrum of effects applied with an impressive variety of tools and methods. You can select the mild texture of a sand finish all the way to a bold stucco effect.

### Ceiling medallions and stenciling
Despite their modest cost, ceiling medallions pack a powerful decorative punch. A properly sized medallion teams up with a ceiling fixture to produce an impressive effect. And a medallion is so easy to install that you'll almost feel guilty accepting the compliments you'll receive on its great looks.

If you've ever stenciled with paint, you'll immediately recognize the concept behind dimensional stenciling (sometimes called plaster stenciling). Instead of paint and a brush, you use drywall compound and a knife. Another surprise: This effect is much easier than stenciling with paint.

### Fastening into drywall
After you've invested all the time and energy to complete your walls, drilling openings for drywall anchors may seem like an unholy act. But unless you're content to stare at blank walls, you'll need to create secure anchor points for hanging pictures, mirrors, and shelves. We've covered a wide selection of fasteners so you can pick the one that's just right for your needs.

## These finishing touches add extra charm and style—and hide mistakes.

### CHAPTER PREVIEW

**Textures for walls and ceilings**
*page 120*

**Installing a ceiling medallion**
*page 124*

**Drywall stenciling**
*page 126*

**Anchoring into drywall**
*page 128*

*Whatever the style of your home, you'll find a complementing ceiling medallion.*

# TEXTURES FOR WALLS AND CEILINGS

Textures add interest, variety, and style to walls and ceilings. A soft spray-on texture that's used exclusively on ceilings is sometimes called "popcorn" or "cottage cheese." Contractors love it because it's faster (and therefore less expensive) than a ceiling that's carefully sanded. And although you can skip the sanding, don't get careless about filling seams and covering the fastener heads. Such defects will show through the texture—especially under critical lighting situations.

To shoot on popcorn texture, you'll need a compressor and must buy or rent a hopper. When you're ready to buy bags of texture, you'll find that there are several sizes of granules. As a rule of thumb, avoid bulky textures in a small room—the texture can become too dominant, making the room seem even smaller.

You can spray thinned-down joint compound through an airless spray rig to create a range of textures on walls and ceilings. But not all applications require fancy equipment. Brooms, sponges, toothed trowels, flat trowels, and other tools yield an unlimited variety of textures. Experiment on scrap pieces of drywall to perfect your technique. Closet ceilings are also a good location to practice techniques.

## PRESTART CHECKLIST

☐ **TIME**
You can spray the ceiling of an average room (12×15) in 15 minutes or less

☐ **TOOLS**
Compressor and hopper

☐ **SKILLS**
Mixing texture material, operating a spray rig

☐ **PREP**
All ceiling seams are flat and smooth; fastener heads properly covered

☐ **MATERIALS**
Texture material, drinking-grade water, ½-inch drill with mixer

## Spraying popcorn ceiling texture

**1** Buy a roll of painter's plastic—a thin, economical translucent sheet—and use masking tape to secure it within 2 inches of the ceiling. Top the plastic with 6-inch-wide masking paper taped along the ceiling/wall joint. A handheld masking machine dispenses half of the tape's width onto the paper. For best results, first paint the ceiling with a primer.

**2** Mix the powdered texture with water according to the manufacturer's directions. Pour a small amount into the hopper, and experiment with different spray tips or pressure settings until you get the desired results. Fill the hopper to a comfortable level (half or less until you get the hang of it), and you're ready to start.

## Caution: Drywall may sag

The moisture—plus the added weight of the texture—can sometimes cause panels to sag noticeably. Before you apply a texture onto a ceiling, verify the thickness of the drywall, the joist spacing, and the application direction of the panels to avoid potential problems. Refer to the Maximum Frame Spacing chart on *page 45* for guidelines.

## Paint-on texture

You can purchase a box of texturing additive and mix it with ordinary paint to achieve a variety of looks without the expense of application equipment. Choose from textures that range from slightly sandy to popcorn. With the larger particles, it can be a challenge to get a consistent appearance over the entire surface. As you work, regularly stir the paint to keep the texture evenly suspended.

## Spraying knockdown texture

**3** Maintain a consistent distance from the ceiling—somewhere between 2 and 4 feet works for most professionals. Walk sideways to spray the first stripe of texture, then slightly overlap it with the second stripe. Continue until you reach the end of the room. Apply the second coat at right angles to the first.

**1** Prime the ceiling to prevent uneven drying of the texture (either water- or solvent-based primer is fine.) Thin all-purpose joint compound with water until it's about the consistency of latex paint. Experiment with an airless paint sprayer on scrap drywall, varying the distance and speed of application until you get the result you want. Spray the ceiling with two coats applied at right angles to each other.

**2** Wait until the ceiling has lost the sheen of moisture—about 10 minutes under average conditions. Hold a wide wipedown blade nearly parallel to the ceiling, and very lightly drag it to flatten the tips of the sprayed texture. Vary the direction of the blade on each pass so you don't create a pattern. If you don't have a 24-inch wipedown blade as shown in the photo, use your widest drywall knife

## Protect fixtures and wiring

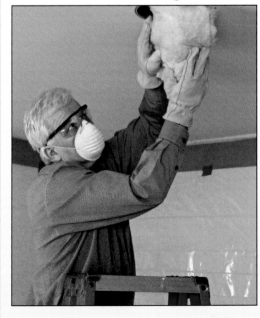

Before applying texture, stuff fiberglass insulation or a wad of newspaper into ceiling canisters. Otherwise, the sprayed material can foul the socket and also make trim rings difficult to install. You can use the same materials to protect wiring in ceiling boxes. Your electrician will thank you because it's a challenge to wire circuits when all of the wires have been sprayed white. For safety, make sure there's no power to electrical boxes in the spray's path.

**STANLEY** PRO TIP

### Dress the part

Safety glasses are an absolute must when you spray a ceiling, and an inexpensive painter's cap is an excellent idea. Long sleeves and full-length pants make personal cleanup easy. Tossing your clothes into the washer is much easier than scraping oversprayed texture from your skin.

# Texture possibilities

**Thin all-purpose joint compound** with water and apply it with a textured paint roller. You may like the effect that comes right from the roller, but you can also knock down the texture for a different look. See Step 2 on *page 121* for a description of the knockdown technique.

**Trowel slightly thinned all-purpose joint compound** onto a wall, then lightly punch it with a brush on a pole to create a texture. The double crow's foot brush in the photo is specifically made for texturing drywall and stucco, but you can experiment with nearly any type of brush. Poke, punch, or drag for a variety of effects.

**Soak a natural sponge in water**, then wring it nearly dry. Experiment with the effects you can achieve by daubing, swirling, punching, and rolling. Frequently change your grip on the sponge to avoid too much regularity.

## Getting into corners

Use a downscaled brush or a fragment of a sponge to continue the texture right into the corner. If you don't finish the corner, your eyes will be drawn to the smooth surface.

## Using texture paint

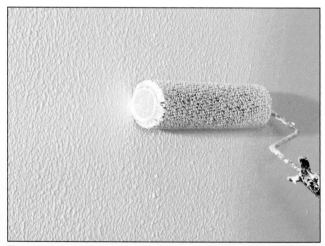

Texture paint isn't a drywall product—you'll find it in the paint aisle of your paint store or home center. You can thin it for application by textured roller or scoop it straight from the tub and handle it like drywall compound to create a wide range of textures. It dries much harder than joint compound.

**Virtually any toothed tool** can create texture. Choose from tiling tools that have square or V-grooves in varying depths, or choose a paint-graining comb or even a hair comb with widely spaced teeth. If you can't find a design that pleases you, make your own from wood, plastic, or metal.

**A stucco-type texture** usually requires two coats of unthinned all-purpose joint compound. Make the first coat just thick enough to create some tool marks. After it dries, apply the second coat with a flat trowel, placing random irregular dabs of material with a skipping motion. Lightly float the trowel over the dabs to flatten them.

## Bold plaster texture

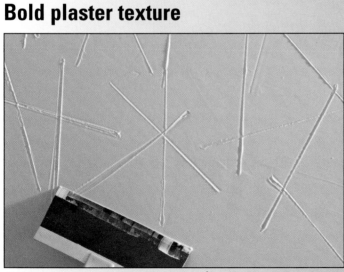

**1** Using a 10-inch drywall knife, apply a ⅛-inch coat of all-purpose joint compound with random sweeping strokes. Then tap the tip in and out of the mud, creating ridges. Overlap your strokes, and work in all directions.

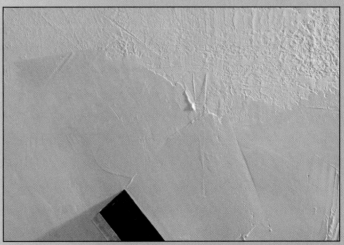

**2** Gently float the knife over the surface to flatten the ridges but not disturb the low areas. Again work randomly to avoid a patterned appearance. Apply compound to the next section of wall or ceiling, overlapping into the completed area for a seamless look.

# INSTALLING A CEILING MEDALLION

Lightweight cast polyurethane mimics the expensive handcrafted look of plaster ceiling medallions found in palaces and mansions. But you don't need a title or an inheritance to add this decorative touch to your home. In fact, it's a quick and affordable do-it-yourself project.

If you don't feel confident with the electrical phase of the job, hire an electrician or purchase a split medallion that doesn't require the fixture's removal.

Follow the sizing guidelines so that your ceiling medallion and light fixture work together as a team instead of competing for attention. Of course, you can install a central medallion in your room even if there's no ceiling fixture. Another popular design idea is to place one large medallion in the center of a big room and position a smaller coordinating medallion near each corner.

There are many other cast elements that you can add to your room: crown moldings, fireplace surrounds, door trim kits, and niches. See "Resources" on *page 139* for some popular sources.

## PRESTART CHECKLIST

☐ **TIME**
Allow one hour if you need to remove and replace a ceiling fixture

☐ **TOOLS**
Tape measure, wire nuts and electrical tape, stiff brush, caulking gun, drill/driver

☐ **SKILLS**
Measuring, caulking, drilling

☐ **PREP**
Remove ceiling fixture

☐ **MATERIALS**
Premium paintable siliconized latex caulk, trimhead screws, nonshrinking filler or surfacing compound

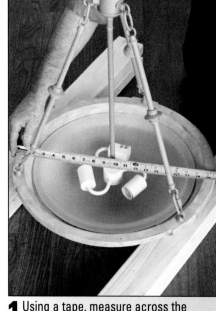

**1** Using a tape, measure across the ceiling fixture to determine its diameter. Choose a medallion with a diameter that is about the same or is slightly smaller. If you use too big a medallion, it will dwarf your fixture instead of complementing it.

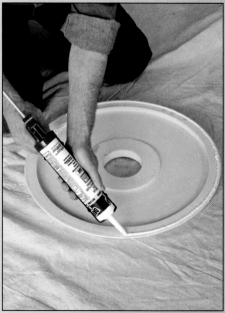

**2** With your caulking gun, lay down a ¼-inch bead of paintable siliconized latex caulk on the backside of the medallion near its rim. Locate and lightly mark ceiling joists.

**STANLEY** PRO TIP

### Removing texture improves adhesion

Loose "popcorn" ceiling texture isn't a reliable anchor for adhesive caulk. Draw the perimeter of the medallion on the ceiling with a pencil, then use a stiff brush to scrub away loose particles of texture.

WHAT IF...
### You don't want to remove the fixture?

Taking down heavy ceiling fixtures could be more than your back or electrical experience permits. In that case, consider a split-ring medallion that slides beneath the fixture's canopy—the metal trim that's snug against the ceiling. With some canopies, you simply loosen a nut to move the canopy downward. Another alternative is a ceiling ring, a donut-shaped medallion that you may be able to install without taking down the fixture.

**3** Press the medallion to the ceiling, and secure it with several trimhead screws. Try to drive at least a couple into ceiling joists. No pilot holes are necessary for the fasteners. Locate the screws in textured areas of the design to help conceal them. Slightly countersink the screws.

**4** Fill the holes with nonshrinking filler or surfacing compound, and sand them smooth after it dries. Wipe away any excess caulk that oozed out at the perimeter of the medallion. For a seamless look, smooth the caulk at the joint between the medallion and the ceiling with a damp fingertip.

**5** Finish the medallion with latex or oil-based paint. If you want a faux finish such as antique brass, you'll find that it's much easier to apply before you install the medallion.

## WHAT IF...
## You don't have a ceiling fixture?

If you want the look without the fixture, purchase a rosette that coordinates with your medallion and use it to cover the central hole. You'll find the rosettes at retailers that sell ceiling medallions.

## A dome adds high drama

A ceiling dome adds a spectacular architectural feature, but its installation requires careful planning at the framing stage of your project. Domes can require a considerable recess—a depth of $6\frac{1}{2}$ inches for a 36-inch diameter is one typical size.

As an alternative to a true dome, consider a surface-mounted medallion with a sweeping interior that gives the illusion of more depth than it actually has.

# DRYWALL STENCILING

The easy decorative process shown here is sometimes called plaster stenciling, but that name is not completely accurate because it's actually accomplished with drywall compound.

Some stencils are a single-layer design; others require multiple applications to achieve full effect. Fortunately it's easy to line up succeeding layers by using the registration holes in the edges of the stencils.

If you don't want to change the design's color from the white of the drywall compound, you can protect it from dirt by spraying or brushing on a coat or two of shellac. This clear finish is compatible with most wall finishes and should not cause a problem when you want to repaint your wall in the future.

An alternative to using white drywall compound is to color a batch of it before application. Look for bottles of universal tints at the paint store that are compatible with water-based products. The color will probably lighten significantly when the compound dries, so experiment until you get the shade you want.

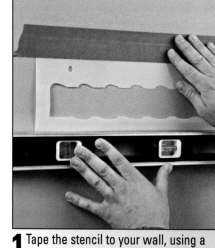

**1** Tape the stencil to your wall, using a level to make certain that it's either level or plumb. If you're using a design that requires several applications, put a pencil point through the punched holes on the stencil's edge to draw registration circles onto the wall.

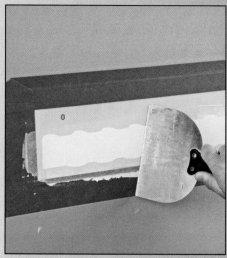

**2** Keeping the stencil flat, fill the recessed areas of the stencil with all-purpose joint compound applied with a drywall knife. For the crispest results, scrape the stencil clean with your knife, leaving the compound only in the open areas.

## PRESTART CHECKLIST

☐ **TIME**
The project time depends upon the amount of area to be covered; multi-layer designs require at least a day between applications

☐ **TOOLS**
Precut stencils, level, tape measure, drywall knife

☐ **SKILLS**
Using a level, aligning registration marks, spreading drywall compound

☐ **PREP**
Wall is completed and painted

☐ **MATERIALS**
All-purpose joint compound, masking tape

## Plaster: from small to XXL, soft to hard

If you need only a small amount of plaster, buy a carton of plaster of Paris at a hardware store or hobby shop. But if you are going to get serious about casting, head to a building supply yard that sells molding plaster. You may find that a 100-pound sack is the only size, but the per-pound price will be dramatically less than for small containers.

Ordinary plaster produces ornaments that are relatively soft. That's acceptable when the medallions are attached to the ceiling or high on a wall. But if the ornament will be subject to impact or abrasion, upgrade to a tougher casting compound. Your local hobby store should be a good source for both information and materials.

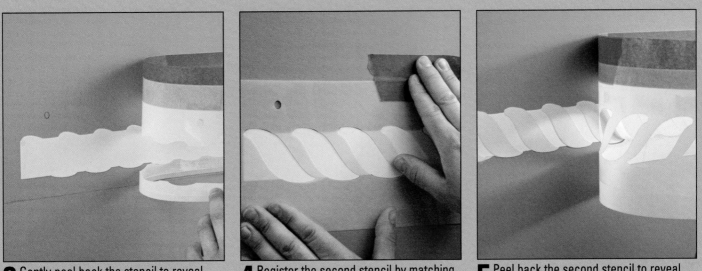

**3** Gently peel back the stencil to reveal the design. Allow plenty of time for the application to dry thoroughly before adding the next layer. If you make a mistake, simply scrape the wet compound off the wall and try again.

**4** Register the second stencil by matching the holes along its edge to the circles you drew on the wall in Step 1, then tape it in place. Repeat the process of filling the stencil with drywall compound and wiping it clean.

**5** Peel back the second stencil to reveal the completed design. After it dries completely, you can prime and paint it, if desired. A "drybrush" painting technique is especially effective in accentuating the plaster design.

## Pouring your own medallions

**1** Mix the plaster according to directions on the label, and place the mold on a level surface. A quick spritz of cooking spray serves as a mold release. Pour in the plaster, and smack your fist on the table next to the mold to dislodge air bubbles on the mold's surface. (The bubbles would produce pits that ruin the surface of your casting.) Using a paint stick with a sawing motion, screed the back of the mold to remove excess plaster.

**2** When the plaster is dry, gently flex the rubber mold to remove the castings. Scrape the edges of the casting with a utility knife blade to remove thin pieces of plaster that extend past the edges of the design. In the rare event that you need to sand an edge, choose drywall screen because it won't clog as easily as regular abrasives. Air-dry the medallions for 48 hours, then attach them to your walls or ceiling with joint compound or construction adhesive.

# ANCHORING INTO DRYWALL

**P**ackages of drywall fasteners often refer to terms such as tensile strength, pullout resistance, and shear strength. Here are some quick definitions to help you sort out the terminology.

Tensile strength refers to the greatest force the fastener can withstand along its length before pulling apart. Shear is a force perpendicular to the fastener's long axis. Pullout resistance is relatively self-explanatory but varies according to the thickness and density of the drywall.

The plain truth is that the drywall will fail long before you're able to load the fastener enough to test its strength. So the panel itself is usually the limiting factor—not the fastener. That's why it's wise to make sure at least one support for a towel bar or light-duty shelf lands on a stud.

For safety, never rely on an anchor alone for overhead use, such as hanging plants. Always drive a threaded fastener into a joist for that type of application.

Match the gauge of the screw to the anchor. The gauge is the number before the length. In the example No. 6×1 inch, the gauge is 6 (bigger number, heavier gauge). Use sheet metal screws for maximum holding power. Unlike wood screws, they are threaded along their entire length.

When choosing an anchor, consider whether you'll ever want to remove it completely from the wall. Some anchors withdraw entirely and easily, while others leave parts behind. Still others are virtually impossible to remove without ripping out a chunk of drywall.

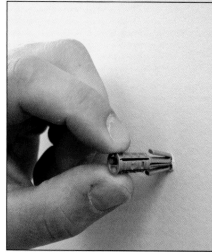

**Expanding plastic anchors** are suitable only for lightweight applications. Be sure you purchase the type of anchor that flares outward behind the drywall for extra holding power. You can sometimes completely remove these anchors without doing too much damage to the wall. But if that's not possible, drive the anchor slightly below the wall's surface, and top with drywall compound.

**Choose an expansion anchor** that has a smooth shank length that matches the thickness of your drywall. Drill the recommended hole size, insert the anchor, and advance the machine screw to expand the legs behind the drywall. Withdraw the machine screw completely, thread it though the item you want to mount, and drive it again. Avoid hammer-in expansion anchors—they often blow out the back of the drywall, weakening or even destroying the gripping surface. Expansion anchors are virtually impossible to remove.

**STANLEY** PRO TIP

### For the most secure anchor, Fasten to framing

Before you start hanging drywall, visualize the location of towel bars, shelves, and heavy pictures or mirrors. Then add 2×4 blocking at all of these locations so that you'll have a solid target for fasteners when you install those accessories later. Fastening into framing is always much stronger than even the best drywall anchor.

### Picture hangers—light duty unless you hit a stud

Simply because the package says "picture hanger" doesn't necessarily mean that the fastener will actually be strong enough to safely hold your picture. Whenever possible, drive the nail into a stud—it will be far more secure than one anchored only into gypsum board.

**Plastic and metal wall drillers** easily auger into your wall with a power screwdriver. To increase pullout resistance, choose a larger diameter anchor. Add a sheet metal screw in the center of the anchor as a mounting point. Removing the driller requires little effort.

**To install a nylon toggle,** simply drill the recommended hole size in the wall, compress the wings, and push the anchor into the hole. The wings usually pop open when they get into the open stud cavity. But if the wings don't expand, insert a slim rod (usually supplied with the anchor) or finishing nail through the anchors to encourage the wings to spread. Removal is virtually impossible.

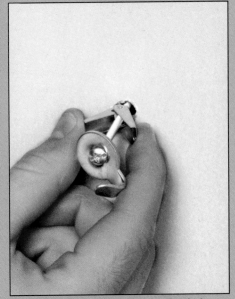

**A toggle bolt** consists of spring-loaded metal wings and a long machine screw. Drill a hole of the recommended size (it's usually stamped on the wings). Put a washer or combination washer and hanger on a long machine screw, spin the wings partially onto the screw, and shove into the wall. Removal is easy—simply back out the screw— although you'll sacrifice the wings.

## Combination washer and hanger

When you use a toggle bolt, you'll need a washer because the hole in the wall is larger than the head of the machine screw. You'll also often need a hook to hang a picture or mirror. Fulfill both needs with the single sturdy piece of hardware shown here. Punching out the scored center ring enables you to use machine screws of several shank diameters.

## Toggle drills its own hole

Toggle bolts are desirable for their strength but undesirable because of the mess and hassle of drilling the entry hole. A new type of fastener called a drywall driller toggle has a self-drilling auger point that makes installation faster and cleaner.

Simply drill the body of the fastener into the wall (Step 1), then begin driving the supplied sheet metal screw (Step 2). As the screw advances (Step 3), it flips the toggle. The screw then engages a hole in the toggle (Step 4) and pulls it snugly against the wall.

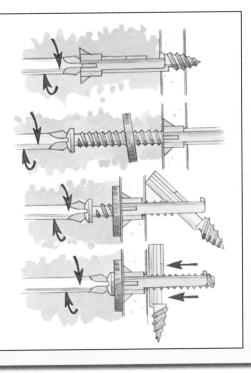

# PATCHING & REPAIRS

In this chapter, you'll learn the step-by-step techniques involved in repairing drywall surfaces to like-new condition. Sometimes the results will be even better than new because you'll correct problems in a way that ensures you won't have to repeat the repair later.

You'll also discover why the problem occurred. That knowledge will help you understand how the repair process works and how to produce a lasting solution.

## Ceiling fixes
Repairing a textured ceiling is an interesting dilemma. If the process works well, it can be a quick one-step repair. But if that first step doesn't pan out, the second becomes a bigger problem, which can then lead to an even larger third step.

The repair is like running down a staircase—missing the first step has serious consequences. The successful repair involves restraint, because spraying too much texture can look more obvious than not quite enough.

Removing the texture from an entire ceiling gives a room a different look. This procedure is a bit messy, but not tedious. The new smooth ceiling is easy to paint and simple to repair.

## Plaster repairs
The plaster walls and ceilings in many older homes can be a mixed blessing. Although a plaster surface is durable, it is subject to cracking and can come loose from the lath and/or the framing.

In some cases you can reattach the plaster and blend the repaired area into the original surface. The step-by-step process, which begins on *page 134,* saves you the time and expense of replacing the entire wall or ceiling.

## Repairing holes and nail pops
Before you paint a room, you should check thoroughly for nail pops. Fixing them is an easy task, and it will improve the appearance of the walls.

Inserting a wall patch is a basic skill you should master. Holes most often are the result of accidental damage, although you sometimes need to cut holes during remodeling projects to pull new wiring or to install other utilities.

---

**Dings and dents are inevitable—and repairable. Simple fixes can renew drywall surfaces.**

## CHAPTER PREVIEW

**Repairing a textured ceiling**
*page 132*

**Repairing loose plaster**
*page 134*

**Repairing a water-damaged ceiling**
*page 135*

**Repairing holes**
*page 136*

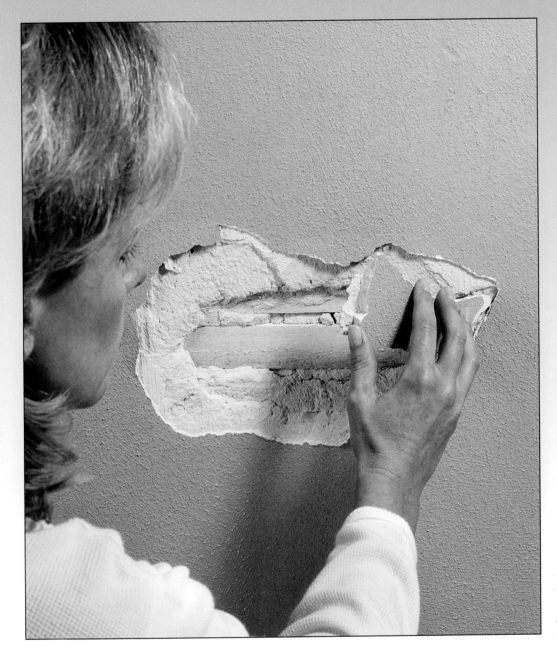

*Drywall techniques also serve to repair damage to plaster walls. The first step is to remove loose pieces of plaster. See page 134 for more about this repair.*

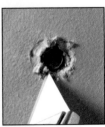

**Fixing nail pops**
*page 138*

# REPAIRING A TEXTURED CEILING

**A** "popcorn" textured ceiling is actually a fragile surface. A good approach to a damaged popcorn texture is to try to ignore the blemish. That's because trying to fix it can lead to even larger problems. If everything goes right, you can be finished in a few minutes. But if something goes wrong, a fix turns into a weekend project.

Aerosol spot-repair products can restore the texture. The trick is to stop before you apply too much texture, making the spot even more noticeable than it was before.

The repaired area will likely dry to a different shade from the rest of the room. Use an aerosol primer to blend the repair into the rest of the surface. The real fix is to clear the room, rent an airless sprayer, and give the entire ceiling a fresh coat of paint.

An alternative is to scrape the texture from the entire ceiling as shown opposite, then prime and paint. It can be a messy job, but the resulting smooth ceiling is easy to repair if it's damaged in the future.

Before working on the ceiling, you may want to have the texture tested for asbestos. Some materials prior to the late 1970s contained asbestos.

## Spot-repair a popcorn texture

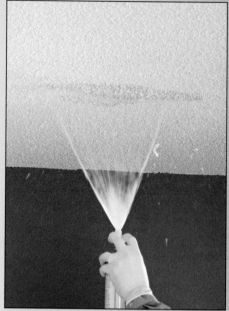

**1** Use a toothbrush to soften the hard edge of the area to be patched. In this case, the damaged area is about 3 inches in diameter. Gently scrape outward with the brush an additional 2 inches, removing only some of the existing texture.

**2** Shoot the texture from the can onto the ceiling in short bursts, blending the new material into the existing texture. Don't overdo the repair—too much texture is as obvious as none at all.

WHAT IF...
### You need to repair only a small area?

Check the paint section of the hardware store or home center and you'll find self-adhesive patches that have a variety of textures. Choose one that matches your wall or ceiling. Carefully scrape away just enough material on the damaged surface for the patch to bond. Press it down thoroughly, then paint the entire ceiling for the best disguise.

**STANLEY** PRO TIP

### Soften the pattern edge

To soften the edge of the texture spray pattern, shoot the material through a hole in a piece of corrugated cardboard held parallel to the ceiling but several inches below it. This technique helps avoid excessive build-up of new texture on areas that don't need it. You can also make the hole with an irregular or scalloped edge to further soften the pattern.

# Removing ceiling texture

**1** Fill a garden sprayer with warm water, adding two or three drops of dishwashing detergent per gallon to improve the wetting power. Mist the ceiling—don't drench it. Wait five minutes and test-scrape a patch. If the texture doesn't release in a single pass, repeat the wetting process.

**2** Scrape off the texture with a drywall knife held at a shallow angle. Position a large dustpan under the scraper to catch most of the material. After you've scraped the ceiling and it's dried, patch any problem areas. Then prime and paint.

## SAFETY FIRST
## Keep your footing

Safety counts when you're doing any operation that gets the floor wet. Heavy plastic sheeting with taped seams will keep finished flooring dry and safe, but you can slip and slide on the slick surface. Top the plastic with sheets of corrugated cardboard to absorb the moisture and keep you on a firm footing.

## Use a step ladder for sure footing

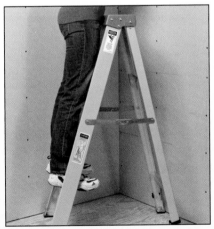

Don't use chairs, benches, or buckets to give yourself a lift when working on a ceiling. A stepladder is much safer.

# REPAIRING LOOSE PLASTER

**B**efore you jump into a plaster repair, learn a little about how the plaster was applied when your house was built. That way, you'll understand how it came loose and what you need to accomplish to fix it.

When the plasterer pushed some of the first coat through the spaces between the lath boards, it oozed behind the strips, creating "keys" that lock the plaster to the strips. Impact or other damage can break the keys, and the plaster can sag from the ceiling or bulge on the wall. Then it's likely to crack.

In a repair job, your first task is to create a new mechanical bond between the surface plaster and the supporting framework. Using special plaster repair washers and screws, attach loose plaster to joists and studs where possible and to lath where necessary.

After you've secured the plaster, the repair proceeds essentially like a drywall finishing project: filling gaps with setting-type compound, embedding tape, and sanding to a smooth surface.

**1** Remove any loose chips from the hole. Mark the location of joists or studs. Put plaster repair washers onto screws and drive the screws into framing lumber or lath surrounding the hole. Press the plaster firmly so the screw will pull it tight. To prevent cracking, drill pilot holes through the plaster using a carbide-tipped drill bit.

**2** Fill the hole with a batch of setting-type joint compound but don't cover the screws and washers yet. Be sure that the patch doesn't bulge past the surface of the plaster. Scratch grooves in the compound to give the next coat of compound a firm grip.

## PRESTART CHECKLIST

☐ **TIME**
The project time depends upon the size of the repair; you also need to allow setting and drying time for the compounds

☐ **TOOLS**
Stud finder, drill/driver, drywall mud pan and knife, utility knife

☐ **SKILLS**
Using a stud finder, driving screws, applying tape and joint compound

☐ **PREP**
Remove loose plaster chips, locate studs or joists

☐ **MATERIALS**
Plaster repair washers with screws, drywall tape, setting-type and premixed compounds, sanding screen

### WHAT IF...
**You need to patch a large area of damaged plaster?**

To speed the repair of large-scale holes, cut a piece of drywall that matches the thickness of the damaged plaster. Glue the patch to the lath and you'll minimize the number of fasteners needed, although you'll still need to drive screws into the framing members for extra security. You don't need to get a perfect fit around the edges because you can fill the voids with setting-type compound. To complete the repair, apply tape over the edges of the patch. Apply feathered layers of compound.

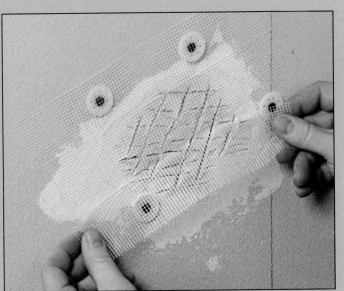

**3** Cover the screwheads and patch with strips of self-adhesive fiberglass tape laid edge to edge. Apply three coats of joint compound, feathering the edges further outward with each application to blend the patch into the surface. Sand, prime, and paint to complete the repair.

# REPAIRING A WATER-DAMAGED CEILING

Repairing the surface damage caused by water is only part of your concern. The more serious problem may be insulation that lost its effectiveness by getting wet, or trapped moisture that could breed mold and invite insect infestation. If any of the drywall feels soft, cut it back to solid material and let the wall cavity dry completely before patching in a new panel. Even if the wall feels solid, cut a 4-inch-square hole into each stud or joist bay to ensure that concealed moisture can evaporate.

WHAT IF...
## You miscut an opening for an electrical outlet?

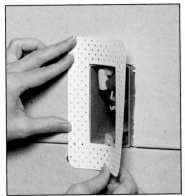

Even experienced drywallers sometimes miscut openings for outlets and ceiling fixtures, but there's products that makes the repair easy. A perforated patch (see "Resources" on *page 139*) is cut to fit a standard single-gang outlet or switch box. First, spread a ¼-inch-thick layer of joint compound on the back of the patch, then press it against a clean and lightly sanded surface. Smooth out the joint compound that oozes through the holes and feather the edges. A second coat is usually enough to blend the patch into the wall.

To repair double-gang boxes or holes for ceiling canisters, cut an opening in a sheet of repair material. Some patches have the outlines of commonly used shapes printed right on the sheet.

## Applying a "hot" patch

Some drywallers like this technique because it eliminates the installation of supports for the patch. Cut the patch about 3 inches larger than the opening it will cover and score lines on the back of the drywall 1½ inches from each edge with a utility knife. Snap the board, but instead of cutting the face paper, carefully peel the

gypsum core from the face paper. After cleaning any remaining gypsum from the paper, test-fit the patch. To install it, smear drywall compound around the hole's perimeter and firmly press the face paper into it. Use a drywall knife to remove excess compound. Two or three feathered coats of compound complete the repair.

# REPAIRING HOLES

**W**hen you consider that drywall covers the vast majority of your home's walls and ceilings, it's almost inevitable you'll occasionally need to fill a hole. Sometimes the culprit is a doorknob, or a playful youngster—or both. A protective doorknob medallion that sticks or screws onto the wall can hide and prevent this kind of dent. Even in new home construction it's quite possible that at least one wall will have a patch before it's had its first coat of paint.

You'll simplify the repair process by making the patch first, then tracing its outline onto the wall. When you cut the hole, you know the patch will fit. Reversing the procedure results in a tedious trial, error, and more error sequence.

Home centers or hardware stores also stock a variety of drywall patches that can speed the repair. Some patches have a self-adhesive back; others must be embedded into joint compound.

It's a good idea to patch holes promptly. If you wait until a day before guests arrive, you probably won't have enough drying time for the coats of compound and touch-up paint.

## PRESTART CHECKLIST

☐ **TIME**
Allow one-half hour to insert the patch and apply the first coat of compound

☐ **TOOLS**
Square, utility knife, saw to cut plywood strips, jab saw, drill/driver, joint compound, mud pan, drywall knife

☐ **SKILLS**
Cutting drywall, driving screws, applying tape and joint compound

☐ **PREP**
Put down a dropcloth to protect finished flooring

☐ **MATERIALS**
Plywood strips, screws, scrap drywall panel for patch material, drywall tape

**1** The first step in repairing an irregular hole is to square up the opening. Cut a square patch slightly larger than the damaged area, and trace its outline onto the wall. Penciled marks on the wall and patch ensure that you'll put it in the same position when you fasten it later.

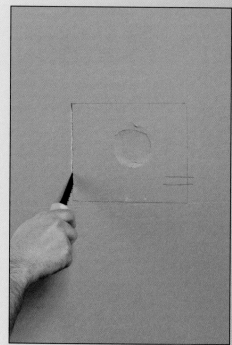

**2** Use your jab saw to cut along the penciled perimeter. Cut just to the outside of the line to create a bit of clearance for the edges of the patch so you won't have to force it into place.

## WHAT IF...
### You don't have wood strips to attach a patch?

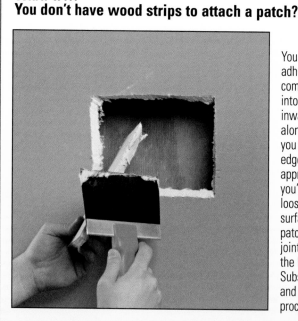

You can take advantage of the adhesive property of drywall compound to bond a tapered plug into the hole. To do this, create an inward bevel of about 45 degrees along the hole's perimeter when you square it. Then rasp down the edges of the patch to an approximate matching hole. When you're satisfied with the fit, brush loose particles from the mating surfaces of both the hole and patch, and "butter" the edges with joint compound. Push the plug into the hole, and tape the edges. Subsequent coats of compound and sanding follow the usual procedures.

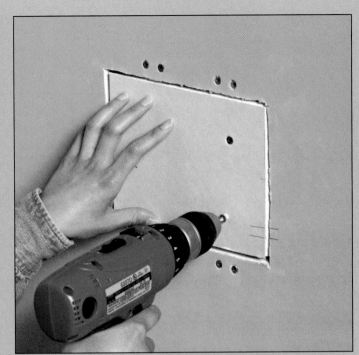

**3** Cut 2-inch-wide strips of ¾-inch plywood about 3 inches longer than the hole's biggest dimension. Slip a strip through the hole, center its width along the opening, and screw it into position.

**4** Screw the patch to the plywood strips. For large-scale holes, put strips around the entire perimeter of the hole. Apply tape over the edges of the patch, then apply three feathered coats of joint compound to blend the repair to the wall's surface. Sanding and painting complete the process.

**STANLEY** PRO TIP

### Use a self-stick patch

For a fast patch, consider a self-adhesive sheet of perforated metal or plastic. Trim it to size, if necessary, strip off the backing, and press it into place. No taping is necessary, so you can immediately apply the first coat of joint compound. For a super-sturdy repair, patch the hole using the procedure at the top of *page 136*, and top it with a self-adhesive sheet.

**WHAT IF...**
### You need to paint a water-damaged ceiling?

Water dripping from the ceiling will often leave an unsightly brown spot or ring. As long as the texture is still firmly attached to the ceiling, you may be able to do a spot repair with stain-blocking primer. Follow label directions for the brand of primer you purchase. Misting the primer away from the center of the spot may help disguise any color mismatch. If the repair is a brighter color than the rest of the room, you may need to paint the entire ceiling. Apply an oil-based paint by using a light touch on your paint roller. Don't use a roller to apply latex paint; because it is water-base, it will loosen the "popcorn" texture and the roller will displace it. Rent or purchase an airless sprayer, and you can apply latex or oil paints.

# FIXING NAIL POPS

**N**ail pops are an annoyance that can ruin the appearance of an otherwise smooth wall. Fortunately they are quite easy to fix. Pity the unfortunate homeowner who finds dozens of them throughout the house on both walls and ceilings.

The usual reason for a nail pop is framing lumber with a moisture content that is too high. During installation, the nail has a good grip on the wood. But as the lumber dries, it shrinks away from the drywall, which has the effect of pulling the nail out of the wood. Any pressure on the drywall panel—which now is no longer in contact with the framing—pushes the nail head against the compound concealing it, creating a mound.

The situation will be even worse if the original drywall hanger hung the panel loosely. For best results, you should always press the panel firmly against the framing with one hand while driving the fastener with the other.

A strong light glancing across the surface will help you quickly see nail pops. You'll also probably discover that the original installer drove the nails in a regular pattern. Screws can also pop, although much less frequently. Please see the fastener selection guide on *page 77.*

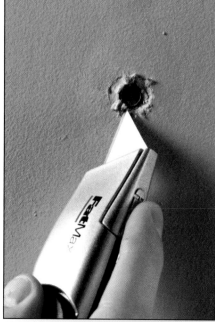

**1** Dig the joint compound out of one mounded area; you'll find the head of a fastener (usually a nail). Position a new ringshank nail next to the head of the old fastener and drive it with a drywall hammer. The rounded head of the hammer will smash the mound into a dimple.

**2** To fix other nail pops, position the new nail slightly off the centerpoint of the mound and drive it to capture the head of the popped fastener. When you nail, push the drywall firmly against the stud or joist.

## PRESTART CHECKLIST

☐ **TIME**
Driving the nail and applying the first coat of compound may take 10 seconds or less per pop

☐ **TOOLS**
Drywall hammer, mud pan with drywall knife

☐ **SKILLS**
Driving nails, applying compound

☐ **PREP**
Move furniture away from walls and remove pictures and other accessories

☐ **MATERIALS**
Drywall nails, all-purpose compound

### WHAT IF...
### You need to fix a crack along an outside corner?

A hairline crack parallel to an outside corner is usually caused by a too-thick application of compound. The stresses of uneven drying

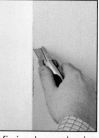

produce a crack. The fix involves enlarging the crack with a utility knife and applying a fresh coat of joint compound. For better insurance against a repeat of the crack, dig out even more compound and span the repair with joint tape.

**STANLEY** PRO TIP

### To tape or not to tape?

Fixing dents and gashes in drywall is a common job. A common question is whether or not

the repair requires a layer of joint tape. Here's an easy rule of thumb: If the face paper is intact, you can skip the tape. But if the paper is cut or ripped, you'll need to reinforce the area with tape. Paper tape, which is thinner than fiberglass mesh, is usually easier to conceal.

Prep a gashed area by using a utility knife to neatly trim away any snagged face paper, so it won't get in the way of your repair.

# RESOURCE GUIDE

**American Society for Testing and Materials**
100 Barr Harbor Drive, West
Conshohocken, PA 19428-2951
610-832-9500
www.astm.org

**Balmer Architectural Mouldings**
271 Yorkland Blvd.
Toronto, ON, M2J 1S5 Canada
1-800-665-3454
www.balmer.com

**Dietrich Metal Framing**
One Mellon Center
500 Grant Street, Ste. 2226
Pittsburgh, PA 15219
412-281-2805
www.dietrichmetalframing.com

**Gypsum Association**
810 First St., NE #510
Washington DC, 20002
202-289-5440
www.gypsum.org

**Magna Industries**
PO Box 734
Lakewood, OH 44107
216-251-3334
www.sandkleen.com
*Dustless sanding system*

**Pittcon Industries**
6409 Rhode Island Ave.
Riverdale, MD 20737
301-927-1000
www.pittconindustries.com
*Raised panel drywall, molding, bead*

**Strait-Flex International, Inc.**
3851 Corporate Centre Drive
St. Charles, MO 63304
636-300-1411
www.straitflex.com
*Drywall patches, flexible bead, X Crack*

**Wilco Drywall Tools, Inc.**
P.O. Box 289
Lewisberry, PA 17399
1-888-292-1002
www.wilcotools.com

**Zipwall LLC**
37 Broadway Suite 2
Arlington, MA 02474
1-800-718-2255
www.zipwall.com
*Dust barrier*

# GLOSSARY

**Back blocking:** The use of a manufactured or homemade device to draw back the untapered ends of drywall panels to provide clearance for drywall tape and compound. Back blocking helps avoid a bulge at a butt seam.

**Backerboard:** Cement or gypsum-based sheets used as substrate for setting tile. See cement board.

**Bead:** An impact-resistant angle (made of metal, composite, or vinyl) that provides mechanical protection at an outside drywall corner and also guides the application of drywall compound to form a crisp junction between the two drywall surfaces.

**Blocking:** Pieces of lumber nailed horizontally between wall studs to serve as anchor points for molding or cabinetry. Blocking also is installed between floor joists to stiffen the floor or to provide a nailing surface for the top of a wall.

**Blowout:** An irregular break, usually at the edge of a drywall panel or along an opening where a portion of the gypsum core detaches from the panel.

**Bullnose:** An edge treatment consisting of a smooth radius.

**Butt seam:** The junction of two untapered drywall ends or edges.

**Cement board:** A type of backerboard made from a cement base and coated or impregnated with fiberglass mesh.

**Coffered:** A type of ceiling construction consisting of one or more stepped surfaces.

**Composite:** An engineered plastic material that's utilized to make inside and outside corners. Heavy-duty composite beads are supplied in fixed lengths.

**Control joint:** A drywall accessory, usually made of metal or plastic, which permits the movement of framing and drywalled surfaces without cracking of the drywall or other damage.

**Cripple stud:** A short stud. Most typically used above door openings in nonbearing walls and below window openings.

**Drywall clips:** A sheet metal device that secures by friction to the edge of a drywall panel and is screwed through a flange to the framing. Drywall clips are often used in the construction of floating ceiling joints at the junction of two walls or a wall and a ceiling.

**Drywall knife:** A tool used for applying and smoothing drywall compound.

**Feathering:** The process of tapering the edge of an application of drywall compound so that its thickness gradually diminishes.

**Fire wall:** A specialized type of wall or ceiling construction utilizing specific materials and techniques designed to inhibit the spread of fire within a structure.

**Floating joint:** A drywall junction that is fastened in a manner so that the framing can move independently of the panel. The technique helps prevent cracked joints.

**Furring strips:** Strips of wood attached to a surface as spacers/anchor points for an additional wall surface. Basement walls often have furring strips added to provide a place to attach drywall. Often made from 1x2s or 1x3s.

# GLOSSARY *(continued)*

**Greenboard:** A moisture-resistant drywall product made for wet installations, such as bathrooms. Greenboard is not waterproof.

**Hanging:** The process of fastening drywall panels to framing.

**J-bead:** A molding made to cover the edge of a drywall sheet so the raw edge does not show in the finished installation.

**Knockdown:** A finishing technique in which a tool such as a drywall knife, trowel, or squeegee is lightly dragged across an application of texturing material to flatten sharp peaks.

**L-bead:** A metal or plastic drywall molding utilized to neatly terminate an edge.

**Mil:** A measurement of thickness equal to one one-thousandth of an inch.

**Mud:** In the construction business, any of a number of wet materials which harden when they dry (such as mortar). In interior work, mud usually refers to the joint compound used to fill the nail holes and seams in drywall.

**Nail pops:** Places in finished drywall where a nail has begun to back out of the stud (or was never completely driven home). Nail pops show up as a small circular lump on the wall surface.

**Off angle:** Any junction between two drywall panels that is not 90 degrees.

**Partition wall:** A wall whose only purpose is to divide a space—it does not contribute to supporting the weight of the building.

**Photographing:** The undesirable visibility of drywall seams after the application of primer. The differing porosities of the compound and the paper surface of the panel cause the effect. Sometimes called ghosting.

**Plate:** A horizontal piece of lumber to which the wall studs are attached. The bottom plate is anchored to the floor. The top plate is usually a double thickness to tie walls together and help carry the load from above.

**Popcorn:** The informal name of a ceiling texture that contains a soft material such as vermiculite to give the installation increased volume at a low weight. Also called cottage cheese.

**Powder-actuated fastener:** A hardened nail that's shot into a dense material such as concrete or metal by the explosive force of a cartridge. The cartridges (called boosters) are available in a variety of strengths to meet the requirements of various target materials.

**Resilient channel:** A metal strip attached to framing and to which drywall panels are secured. Resilient channels are utilized for sound control purposes or as furring strips (also see that entry).

**Ring shank:** A series of annular ridges around the shaft of a nail designed to increase its pullout resistance. This is a effective design for drywall nails.

**Runner:** The C-shape sheet metal track that serves as the top and bottom plate in metal stud construction. Also called track.

**SAFB** (Sound Attenuation Fire Blanket): A semi-rigid mineral wool insulation material that provides benefits in blocking both sound and fire.

**Scribe:** The process of making an item, such as shelf or countertop, conform to the irregularities of another surface—such as a wall—in order to achieve a fit without gaps.

**Shim:** A strip of wood, usually tapered, employed as a filler to create a solid surface between two elements. For example, pairs of tapered softwood shims take up the space between a door jamb and the rough framing of an opening so that the two can be joined solidly.

**Skim coating:** The process of covering the entire surface of a drywall installation with a paint-thin layer of joint compound in order to produce a uniform porosity. This treatment helps prevent photographing (also see that entry).

**Soffit:** An enclosed architectural feature, usually at the junction of a wall and ceiling, which is sometimes utilized to fill the space that would otherwise occur between the top of wall-mounted cabinets and the ceiling. The enclosed space may be utilized for light fixtures, wiring, heat ducts, and other utilities. Sometimes called a bulkhead.

**STC** (Sound Transmission Class): A method of quantifying the effectiveness of an architectural system in preventing the passage of sound. The higher the STC number, the more effective the system.

**Stud:** The vertical members of a house's frame. Often made from 2×4s or 2×6s.

**Stud bay:** The space between two studs installed in a wall.

**Tapered edge:** the long edges of drywall sheets usually have their thickness gradually reduced in order to permit the embedding of drywall tape without developing a bulge.

**Substrate:** any of several layers, including the subfloor, beneath a tile surface.

**Taping:** Describes the process of applying paper or mesh tape to drywall joints in preparation for application of joint compound.

**Trim-head screw:** A design of screw with an extremely small head; useful as a fastener for attaching moldings while producing a minimal hole to be filled.

**Trowel:** A tool used for applying and smoothing drywall compound. The trowel design usually has the handle parallel to the working surface; similar to the shape of concrete-finishing tools.

# INDEX

# INDEX *(continued)*

## METRIC CONVERSIONS

| U.S. Units to Metric Equivalents | | | Metric Units to U.S. Equivalents | | |
|---|---|---|---|---|---|
| To convert from | Multiply by | To get | To convert from | Multiply by | To get |
| Inches | 25.4 | Millimeters | Millimeters | 0.0394 | Inches |
| Inches | 2.54 | Centimeters | Centimeters | 0.3937 | Inches |
| Feet | 30.48 | Centimeters | Centimeters | 0.0328 | Feet |
| Feet | 0.3048 | Meters | Meters | 3.2808 | Feet |
| Yards | 0.9144 | Meters | Meters | 1.0936 | Yards |
| Square inches | 6.4516 | Square centimeters | Square centimeters | 0.1550 | Square inches |
| Square feet | 0.0929 | Square meters | Square meters | 10.764 | Square feet |
| Square yards | 0.8361 | Square meters | Square meters | 1.1960 | Square yards |
| Acres | 0.4047 | Hectares | Hectares | 2.4711 | Acres |
| Cubic inches | 16.387 | Cubic centimeters | Cubic centimeters | 0.0610 | Cubic inches |
| Cubic feet | 0.0283 | Cubic meters | Cubic meters | 35.315 | Cubic feet |
| Cubic feet | 28.316 | Liters | Liters | 0.0353 | Cubic feet |
| Cubic yards | 0.7646 | Cubic meters | Cubic meters | 1.308 | Cubic yards |
| Cubic yards | 764.55 | Liters | Liters | 0.0013 | Cubic yards |

*To convert from degrees Fahrenheit (F) to degrees Celsius (C), first subtract 32, then multiply by ⁵⁄₉.*

*To convert from degrees Celsius to degrees Fahrenheit, multiply by ⁹⁄₅, then add 32.*

# KNOWLEDGE IS THE BEST TOO

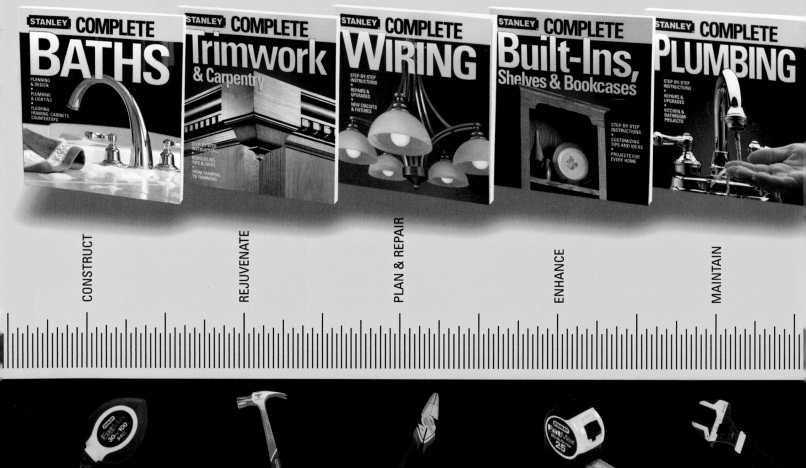

STANLEY COMPLETE **BATHS**
PLANNING & DESIGN
PLUMBING & LIGHTING
FLOORING, FRAMING, CABINETS, COUNTERTOPS

STANLEY COMPLETE **Trimwork & Carpentry**
STEP-BY-STEP INSTRUCTIONS
REMODELING, TIPS & IDEAS
FROM FRAMING TO TRIMMING

STANLEY COMPLETE **WIRING**
STEP-BY-STEP INSTRUCTIONS
REPAIRS & UPGRADES
NEW CIRCUITS & FIXTURES

STANLEY COMPLETE **Built-Ins, Shelves & Bookcases**
STEP-BY-STEP INSTRUCTIONS
CUSTOMIZING TIPS AND IDEAS
PROJECTS FOR EVERY HOME

STANLEY COMPLETE **PLUMBING**
STEP-BY-STEP INSTRUCTIONS
REPAIRS & UPGRADES
KITCHEN & BATHROOM PROJECTS

CONSTRUCT     REJUVENATE     PLAN & REPAIR     ENHANCE     MAINTAIN

LOOK FOR THESE EXCITING HOME IMPROVEMENT
TITLES WHEREVER BOOKS ARE SOLD

**STANLEY**®
MAKE SOMETHING GREAT™